Airborne

Airborne

Neil Williams

Illustrated by Lynn Williams

www.crecy.co.uk

First Published by Airlife Publishing 1977

Reprinted 1978

Reprinted 1981

This second edition published in 2011 by Crécy Publishing Limited

A CIP record for this book is available from the British Library

ISBN 9 781906 559212

Printed and bound in England
by MPG Books Ltd

Crécy Publishing Limited
1a Ringway Trading Estate, Shadowmoss Road, Manchester M22 5LH
www.crecy.co.uk

Contents

Foreword

by Air Commodore Allen Wheeler
CBE MA FRAeS

I HAVE known Neil Williams since he first competed in the Lockheed Aerobatic Trophy Competition, of which I was one of the judges. We knew then that a new 'star' was arising in the aerobatic world. Since then be has flown in films in which I was involved; he now regularly flies for us in the Shuttleworth Trust Collection of historic aeroplanes, and of course takes part regularly in international aerobatic displays and competitions of every kind all over the world. All that is still only a part of the immensely diverse type of flying in which he indulges regularly. Now, to the benefit of the aeronautical bookshelves of all interested in aviation, he has added another book on his experiences in the air, which must be unique.

Airborne is not just an interesting and amusing book to read, but in it Neil clearly illustrates three valuable lessons that cannot be emphasised too often; they apply to seasoned pilots almost as much as to less experienced ones, and all classes of pilots would do well to study them and remember them.

First, Neil frankly admits to mistakes he has made in his flying career; that alone is rare amongst even the best pilots, almost non-existent amongst the worst – and he goes on to show how such errors can occur. Second, he reveals in detail the amount of intense planning and practice that is essential before taking on any display. Third, he shows that engines still fail, structures can still be strained or broken, and pilots should be ready for such eventualities, especially if they aspire to indulge in the sort of up-to-the-limits flying that is described in this book. If a pilot of Neil Williams's ability and experience finds it necessary to concentrate on such considerations, then who in the world can claim he needn't?

His chapter on 'The Big Show' (the SBAC Display) indicates very well how important practice, planning and meticulous timing are, even within seconds if the display is to be safe and effective. There is also the true warning implied never to do more in the actual display than you have done in practice; the perfectionist or aspiring perfectionist will always do the best he can whether the crowd watching be ten or ten thousand.

The chapter on the Heinkel 111 is indeed good reading and records how a good and viceless aeroplane can be given a bad reputation by some other pilots with no justification at all. I have met this situation on many occasions myself, but one still cannot afford to ignore such reports and check them carefully when one first flies that type – as Neil did!

Perhaps the most fascinating chapter of all is the description of the author's immediate thoughts and actions when the wing failed on Zlin during a practice for the World Aerobatic Contest and he had no parachute. His achievement in this case must rank amongst the greatest feats in aviation in an emergency.

Allen Wheeler

March 1977

1

...the exhausts look like twelve blowlamps, the smoke is now arcing outwards, clear of the cockpit, the noise is beyond description, the whole world is full of thunder and she's moving faster...

Spitfire

SPITFIRE! Legendary in its first decade, with a beauty that could only be conceived by a designer who knew that he was dying, that this aeroplane would be his last, and his greatest. A thoroughbred, a direct descendant of the fastest seaplane racers of all time, the S4, S5 and S6. Slender, sleek, with nearly 2,000 horsepower beneath a shark-like cowling, with eight machine guns hidden in her elegant elliptical wings, surely she was the most graceful, beautiful, deadly machine of war ever made. She was called Spitfire, and she lived up to her name. She flew for the first time in the shadow of war, in the spring of 1936. There were those who doubted that such a revolutionary aeroplane would be successful, for these were the days when the biplane fighters reigned supreme. Certainly the monoplanes were faster, but surely they were not sufficiently reliable to go to war; one only had to look at the Supermarine racers, with their overheating problems, and the difficulties of overcoming that much-feared killer, control flutter.

The pessimists were quick to point out that the racing seaplanes had to start their take-off runs across wind, allowing the terrific torque and slipstream effects to align them with the take-off path, even against full opposite rudder. These machines could only be flown by very experienced and skilful pilots – what hope then for the Spitfire with raw young squadron pilots?

And so, on that historic day, 5 March 1936, there assembled a small crowd who waited with bated breath. Mitchell, the designer, a very sick man, was there too, to see the culmination of all his efforts. Dainty and trim in her pale blue paint, she started her take-off crosswind, as did the seaplanes – but to their amazement she ran straight, easily controllable, and lifted effortlessly into her natural element. And it was here that they saw her true beauty, for no one can watch a Spitfire in flight and fail to be entranced. Mitchell himself died only a year later, but his aeroplane was to live on. From prototype to production, increasing Marks saw more power, different armament, more fuel, different canopies, but still the Spitfire retained her lines. And so she went to war.

For a small boy growing up in a tiny Welsh village, the war was remote. Now and then there would be a raid on the coastal installations miles to the south and sometimes aircraft were seen, some ominous, with black crosses, some with graceful wings and slim fuselages with RAF roundels. Even at that tender age the Spitfire had captured my imagination, and my most treasured possession was a model Spitfire, made out of an ordinary penny! For myself and for countless others, the Spitfire was a symbol, for they were emotional times.

The war eventually finished, years passed, and I joined the RAF. To be sure, there was still the occasional Spitfire airworthy, and we looked on these with covetous eyes, for that boyhood longing was still there. Jealously guarded, meticulously maintained, and flown by officers of high rank, what chance was there for an ordinary squadron pilot to fly one, even a quick circuit, just to fly a Spitfire? None, it would seem. It appeared to resemble the question of landing at Gibraltar, a treacherous and unforgiving airfield when there was a crosswind. 'You can't land at Gibraltar unless you've landed there before,' they said! So it was with a Spitfire – 'You can't fly our Spitfire unless you've flown one before!'

But Lady Luck works in mysterious ways! One day at the flying club I noticed an American obviously interested in our old Tiger Moth. It transpired that he had never flown one, so I took him up for a few circuits. It was a foul day, raining, with a gusting crosswind, but he seemed to enjoy it immensely. As we thawed out over coffee, the talk was inevitably of aeroplanes. Real aeroplanes.

'Have you ever flown a Spitfire?' he asked.

'No,' I said, looking at him sideways.

'You can fly mine if you like,' was the reply.

God, I'm dreaming, I thought. But he seemed serious enough. It had apparently been bought in Belgium and was to be flown to Southend by a Belgian, from where it was to be flown to Swanton Morley. Would I like to ferry it? Can a duck swim, I thought! And so it was agreed. I scrounged some Pilot's Notes (it was a Mk IX) and read through them again and again. I talked to people who had flown them until I must have driven them nearly to distraction!

Eventually the great day dawned, and I saw with relief that the forecaster had been right – the weather was perfect. Impatiently I sat in the right-hand seat of a friend's Jodel waiting for Southend to appear. That flight seemed interminable to me, but at last we were on the ground – and there she was! A Spitfire Mk IX, looking trim and efficient in her camouflage paint. She dominated the airport as she stood there, alone and proud, on the tarmac. I could barely wait for the Jodel to stop before I was out, with my parachute slung across my shoulder. For several minutes I just looked at her. This – the ambition of a lifetime – was at last to be satisfied.

But I must be careful – although I was flying jet aircraft regularly, the biggest single piston I had flown before was a Harvard, eight years before. This beauty at full power could reach 1,750 horsepower. I hesitated as I looked at the narrow-tracked undercarriage and the tiny fin and rudder, and I thought of the almost uncontrollable swing on take-off of the Supermarine seaplanes. This Spitfire had almost twice the power of the prototype.

The decision was made for me as a mechanic appeared with a trolley-acc. Trying to look as though I did this sort of thing every day, I swung my parachute onto the tailplane and climbed up onto the wing. I gave the hood a tug – nothing happened. I pulled harder – still it remained tightly closed. I looked for a release catch, but none was visible. The mechanic was not much help either; he was all for pulling what was obviously the hood jettison cable. Now, don't panic, I thought. What a stupid situation, a Spitfire, full of fuel, asking to be flown, and I can't get into it! Inspiration – Pilot's Notes. Quickly I thumbed through – nothing. Again, more thoroughly – still no luck. For the tenth time I examined the canopy, and then I found it – a tiny button, on top of the windscreen arch – and the hood slid open. I installed the parachute and checked the airframe over. I adjusted the seat for height and the pedals for reach – each pedal had an independent screw adjustment.

Trying to look nonchalant, I went up to control to book out. The Spitfire had no radio so I anticipated all kinds of difficulty. But I had reckoned without the aura of sentiment that surrounds this aeroplane. Yes, I could use any runway I wanted to – they would hold all other traffic until I was on my way, and please would I give them an aerobatic display before I left? Somehow I got out of the office without committing myself – I had an idiotic fear that if I left the aeroplane for more than a few minutes somebody else would grab it! I climbed aboard and strapped myself in. I opened the door one notch to hold the canopy locked open, and at last I was ready. My checklist was strapped to my right leg, maps in the correct order were in my left overall pocket, and Pilot's Notes in the right.

Seven shots on the primer and we were ready to go. I switched on the mags, and pressed the starter and booster coil buttons. With a wheeze and a whine that gigantic propeller started to turn, very slowly, kicking back slightly with the gears banging and protesting, and just when I was about to release the buttons and rest the starters it fired! The noise was indescribable, it paralysed thought and action. Acrid black smoke erupted from the exhausts and was slammed backwards. The machine was 'alive' – it trembled and vibrated, it radiated power. Merlin: his modern namesake holds men entranced, spellbound with its mighty music, from the deep vibrating throb through the spectrum of sound to the roaring song of full power. No other engine sounds the same – there is magic in the Merlin.

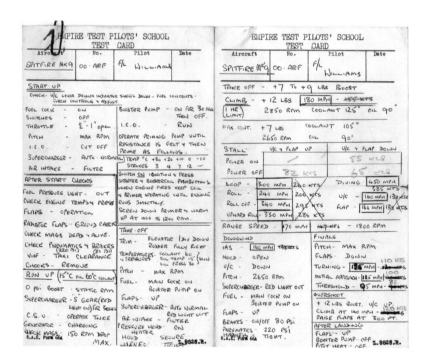

But pay attention! There are things to do: oil pressure – within limits; radiator temperature – rising. I must be quick, or the coolant may boil – but at the same time everything must be checked. I wave the chocks away and release the parking brake and immediately she starts to move. The brakes are relatively weak, but in spite of this the aircraft is 'tail light' and can quite easily be put onto its nose by harsh use of brakes, especially when power is applied. I can see absolutely nothing ahead, and have to swing that enormous nose from side to side as I taxi.

The engine is vast by comparison with other machines, and the huge, geared-down propeller is nearly 10 feet ahead of the cockpit! The tailwheel is free to castor through 360 degrees, and I note with trepidation that even at taxiing speed she is trying to groundloop! With the hood open, exhaust fumes make the eyes sting and smart, so I pull down my goggles. The radiator temperature is rising steadily as I prepare for run-up – there must be no fumbling here. Brakes on, stick back, 1,200rpm, generator charging, and slowly increase power to zero boost, ready to throttle back instantly if the tail starts to lift.

Now the noise is stunning – it is difficult to concentrate – check static rpm – exercise the constant speed unit twice and check magnetos – not more than 150rpm drop. The radiator temperature is nearly 100°C as I throttle back – these big liquid-cooled engines were not intended to run for any length of time on the ground. Quickly I run through the take-off checks, pausing momentarily at 'Rudder trim – FULLY RIGHT', remembering the gigantic torque of the racing seaplanes. A green light from the tower and I cautiously line up in the centre of the runway.

This is it! I release the brakes and gently ease the throttle open. With increasing confidence as she rolls straight I ease the stick forward and apply more power. As the tail starts to come up she swings to the left – full right rudder, but she's still swinging left, so throttle back a bit and put the tail back on the ground. Now she's straightened, so ease the power on again and lift the tail gently, gently. Still full right rudder and some right aileron and now she's accelerating, only just under control, still can't see ahead, snatch a glance at the boost, +4lb increasing, the exhausts look like twelve blowlamps, the smoke is now arcing outwards, clear of the cockpit, the noise is beyond description, the whole world is full of thunder and she's moving faster, she's light on the wheels – and she's flying!

The stick is quivering, it needs a firm grip, she's crabbing to the left as I increase power to +9lb boost, flick the brakes on briefly and release the throttle to change hands on the stick before retracting the undercarriage. As I do so, that devastating soul shattering noise dies to a subdued growl – the throttle has vibrated closed. Quickly I change hands and reapply power. She yaws drunkenly as she surges forward – the directional trim change with power is incredibly large, and my feet are still too heavy for a Spitfire. This must look awful from the ground! I work quickly – stick between knees, tighten throttle friction with the right hand (and I could have sworn it was really tight before I started), change hands again to retract the gear. Push the handle down, pause, inwards, pause, upwards, pause and release, and hope for the best! The handle springs into position and the hydraulic circuit flag shows 'idle'. The word 'UP' is illuminated, and by all this I am led to believe that the undercarriage is up; but I must check the radiator temperature because if one leg is unlocked it will hang in front of the radiator and cause the engine to overheat! During this performance I have been trying to execute a straight climb-out left-handed.

Next is the struggle to close the hood. Remember those newsreel films in the war when the canopies were slid closed in one polished movement? They must have been double-jointed. The noise is less brutal now as the engine note blends with the hiss of the slipstream – suddenly I realise that I am holding left rudder, and I back off the rudder trim. As the foot force disappears I am able to take stock of the situation and suddenly I realise that this aeroplane feels 'right', that one does not turn mechanically, one merely thinks of turning and it is done! In this machine one is immediately at home, it is instantly responsive; touchy as a thoroughbred, it will not allow slipshod flying, even a slightly out-of-balance turn causes the pilot to be ashamed of mishandling such a sensitive beauty.

The elevator trimmer is powerful but the trim curve is fairly flat, so I do not need to make many adjustments. But for every change of power and speed the directional trim change is considerable.

The airfield is spread out below as I turn and remember that I have been asked for some low runs. With the power set at +7lb boost, 2,650rpm, she accelerates rapidly in a shallow dive, and I note that stability in pitch is positive. The ailerons and elevator are well harmonised at intermediate speeds, giving the aeroplane its 'natural' feel. With 250 knots on the clock she races across the field, and as I pull up the exhilaration is too much, and she rolls effortlessly in the climb.

Cruising northwards, the Merlin purring steadily, I am content.

At 10,000 feet East Anglia stretches for miles, as I start to get to know this wonderful aeroplane. The ailerons are crisp, powerful and smooth, so much so that I am reluctant to fly straight and level for long. Chandelles and lazy eights are only the beginning, but I notice that in the dive the ailerons become stiff and heavy. Looping is easy, but requires a light touch on the stick; too much back pressure and she shudders on the edge of a stall. Over

the top she insists on fast accurate footwork to keep straight. It's hot, too, in this tiny cockpit, heavy with the smell of petrol and glycol, and all the things that go to make up a Spitfire cockpit. I try a slow roll, so easy in this aeroplane. It's really 'slow', and the nose-down pitch as rudder comes on in the inverted position is exactly right to keep the nose up without having to press the stick forward. Of the Spitfire, an old wartime acquaintance once said in jest, 'You can't do a really 'slow' roll in a Spitfire, because the fuel endurance is only an hour and a half!'

But now, all too soon, I am nearing my destination – it is time to think of landing. A stall check shows remarkable docility, good warning in the form of elevator buffet 10 knots before the stall, and a gentle nose-down pitch with mild wing drop at the stall itself. The ailerons are effective right down to the stall and the elevator is very powerful. It is not necessary to pull the stick all the way back to stall the aircraft – if this is done the buffeting is heavier and the wing drop is more pronounced. With wheels and flaps down and power off, the Spitfire stalls at 63 knots.

Armed with this information I indulge in some more aerobatics, this time lower down, and finish with some tight turns. At low altitude one can see how incredibly tightly the Spitfire can turn, with only the lightest of stick pressures – no wonder she could out-turn the contemporary fighters of her day! I can feel the 'g' building up, and suddenly realise that the world is going grey – in a 5g turn with a remarkably low stick force – the manoeuvring stability in pitch decreases with increasing 'g'. Better be careful – this could be dangerous low down. Unlike a modern aircraft she has only borderline stability, and she must be 'flown' all the time. A low run-in for a break and as I throttle back the characteristic popping and banging of the exhausts blends with the whistle of the slipstream as I pull up and around onto the downwind leg. I select the undercarriage down, and at the same time increase power to balance the drag. As I slide the canopy back the music of the Merlin at 2,650rpm is loud over the battering slipstream.

I fly a wide circuit and select flaps as I turn base leg. With a hiss of air, they operate instantly, causing an abrupt nose-down trim change. I increase rpm to 2,850 and the deep Merlin note rises to a high-pitched whine as the blades fine off. Speed is reducing to 100 knots as I roll out on final approach, and now I realise my mistake – not only has the runway vanished, I cannot even see the airfield! With her nose up, the Merlin has reduced forward visibility to nil!

Now I know why Spitfire pilots flew those beautiful curved approaches – not to show off, but merely so that they could see where they were going! This time I remember to give the throttle friction a quick twist before smoothly increasing power to +9lb boost. And this time I am ready with right rudder and a touch of right aileron as she starts crabbing to the left. Steady forward pressure with the left hand on the stick as I retract the undercarriage – the pressure increases as the gear comes up and she accelerates, and as she climbs away I trim well forward before selecting flaps up, and she pitches up abruptly as she accelerates. But now I am ready for her tricks and even the prodigious blare of the exhaust and the battering thunder of the slipstream no longer stupefy the senses. Now it is pure exhilaration as this mighty creature responds to the slightest pressure. I marvel at the colossal power instantly commanded at the touch of a lever. Jet flying was never like this!

Again downwind, throttle back, and this time I fly a tight, high circuit. Throttle right back, and keep turning. The Merlin crackles and bangs as, with a touch of rudder and opposite stick, I feed a little sideslip into the turn, just as I did as a student on Tiger Moths. Now I can see everything, and as I cross the hedge I let her straighten. I can no longer see ahead, but now I am over the grass, and that great nose rears up higher and higher as she sinks lower. The elevator is very sensitive and powerful and there is plenty of control, more than I have ever seen on any aeroplane before. There! She touches, on all three points, and now I hold the stick hard back and very gently apply the brakes.

She rolls slower and slower, and I start to relax when, without any warning, she starts to swing to the right. Full left rudder, full brake. Phew! Just in time! The tail is kicking very slightly, warning me that she will not take kindly to any mishandling, even at 10mph. Slowly, I taxi to the hangar, reluctant now to break the spell, for even if I fly this magnificent machine again, it will never be the same as this, my first solo. I stop in front of the hangar and idle for a few seconds at 1,000rpm. I pull the ICO to the fully aft position and, with a final growl, the Merlin slows and stops.

The silence is heavy and oppressive, and this great creature, vibrant with life such a short time ago, now lies lifeless and inert. But still the magic remains; I sit in the cockpit, remembering, savouring every detail. I become aware of people crowding around, and slowly return to reality – I release the harness and the parachute and clamber stiffly to the ground. 'What's it like?' they all want to know, and I reply, 'It was great, marvellous,' knowing all the while that there are no words to describe what I have experienced, for it was not 'just another aeroplane' – this one was different. I have lived with a part of history, and have felt – something. The care, the knowledge, the incredible efforts of a dying man to produce a masterpiece – something was there. I cannot identify it and now it seems distant and hazy – but high in the clean air behind the beat of that powerful engine it felt alive. I know. I was there. In a Spitfire.

2

I felt the grip of fear, I knew I was out of control;
I was afraid to relax the pull on the stick, and
always there was the sensation of looping.

Taught by a Tiger

IN the immediate post-war years, long before the advent of the IMC rating, the business of learning to fly was uncomplicated and enjoyable. Radio in light aeroplanes was a luxury that was indulged in primarily by those few pilots who used their machines for business, and in fact was often more of an expensive nuisance than anything else. If you wanted to go somewhere, you merely went and, on arrival, flew over the top at 2,000 feet and had a look at the signals square.

In those days, 'airliner' circuits were reserved for airliners, and light aeroplanes flew neat small circuits, which would permit a glide landing on the aerodrome in the event of an engine failure. It also allowed all the machines to be easily seen, with the result that there was rarely a need to overshoot. The duty of the controller was to log the movements and to fire a 'red' if he saw a dangerous situation, which he was not often required to do.

Airmanship was the order of the day; one kept one's eyes open, and the whole business was very simple and straightforward.

With no radio or navigational aids on board, it was, of course, necessary to practise map-reading and cross-country flying with some diligence; if you got lost, you really were on your own! Strangely enough, with very little training, and a rudimentary compass, very few of us did get lost, especially by comparison with circumstances today, although I suppose there are more pilots flying light aircraft these days.

There was no instrument training in the PPL syllabus – you just stayed out of cloud at all costs, even if it meant coming back with twigs and leaves in the undercart, or even landing in a field.

I had won a flying scholarship, and had just gone solo on a Tiger Moth. I was in my teens, had 10 hours PI, and of course I thought I knew it all! Not for me the boring ritual of compass courses and map-reading; I was going to teach myself aerobatics!

Of course I would have been grounded had I been caught, but when you are a teenager in an aeroplane that trained thousands of fighter pilots, you don't think of these things. The folly of youth is never realised at the time!

So it was that on a fine summer's evening the little Tiger ran lightly across the grass and lifted easily into the air. The duty – map-reading; the intention – aerobatics.

The flat coastal plain of South Wales spread out below me as I climbed; to the north the ground rose into the rolling hills that were surmounted by the Brecon Beacons. To the south the Bristol Channel, and beyond the coast of Somerset. Now the warm air of the lower levels had given way to the sting of winter as the biting slipstream made me catch my breath. The large industrial towns of the coast were no longer blots on the landscape; as I climbed ever higher they merged with the wide plain and I became aware only of the sea, the land, the mountains – and the clouds.

Ahead of me was a perfect plateau of alto-stratus, flat and smooth, stretching away inland, while above towered snowy mountains of dazzling cumulus cloud, touched with silver and gold, changing shape and colour with every second. It was a scene beyond the imagination – I sat transfixed. Gone were thoughts of aerobatics, time meant nothing, the world below did not exist. Now I was above the stratus level. I revelled in the sensation of power and speed – with no thought of danger I roared across the brilliant plain, brushing its surface with the wheels, as if it was really a frozen world of snow and ice, for so it appeared. And always with me, majestic and awesome, boiled the swirling masses of the giant thunderstorm clouds of summer.

At last I tired of this flat, featureless plain, and I turned the nose of the Tiger towards a vast cleft between two of the largest clouds – what fun it would be to lunge through a canyon bordered by walls of ice, surrounded by colour so unreal that it defied description. I started to climb, but as I drew ever nearer it still towered high above me. Alas for youth's puny spirit of adventure; now, had I but known it, I was making mistake after mistake, a series of errors that, if pursued far enough, could have but one outcome! All unknowing, with my 10 hours solo experience behind me, I pressed on!

Now there was no doubt: the Tiger didn't seem to be climbing properly. Not only had I not allowed for the lower rate of climb at height, but I had forgotten to open the throttle!

The sheer wall of the mountain of cloud suddenly seemed to leap at me; I thought to turn away, but too late. The splendour of that Arctic scene, in all its glory, was wiped out in a flash. Instead I was in a grey world of mist. Now I was conscious of the vulnerability of my frail machine as every vibration and tremor was magnified by apprehension. Now my stupidity came home to me: I must get out, I must go back! I had never before flown in cloud – and because all my instruction had been visual, I had never been shown how to interpret the turn and slip indicator!

I must do something, and quickly; I cannot yet be too far in. A simple turn through 180 degrees. I looked at the meaningless instruments, thrust the stick to the left, and pulled! I felt the 'g' build up, and when I thought I must have turned through 180 degrees I straightened out – or so I thought. The

... with my heart in my throat I saw the altimeter unwind furiously...

ASI showed the speed increasing. I pulled back on the stick. Still the speed rose, in spite of pulling even harder. In rising fright, I closed the throttle, but now the slipstream was screaming in the wires as the 'g' increased.

What was happening? Speed steady at 130mph, throttle closed, stick well back; I had the feeling that I was looping, I no longer had any idea of attitude, and always the high-pitched scream of the slipstream. I looked wildly around the primitive panel, and with my heart in my throat I saw the altimeter unwind furiously, the liquid in the ancient fore and aft inclometer was not even visible, speed still 130. I looked at the turn and slip indicator: its wild reading meant nothing.

Down and down went the Tiger; now the instruments were blurred, condensation had formed not only in them, but also on the glass of my goggles. I felt the grip of fear, I knew I was out of control; I was afraid to relax the pull on the stick, and always there was the sensation of looping.

They say that in times of stress one's life passes before one's eyes; all I could see in my mind's eye was a pathetic pile of crumpled wreckage strewn across a bleak mountain top. Fear gave way to a feeling of nausea; I knew that the end was only seconds away. I felt as though it was all a bad dream – this really wasn't happening to me at all. Nausea was now replaced by apathy, a feeling of 'let's get it over with'.

Now I was looking forward to the expected impact, sure in my mind that I would then wake up at home in bed and discover it really was only a dream. Had I but known it, the mental protection system we all have was saving me from those last few seconds of terror. I sat, numbed, waiting for the end.

Suddenly, with the violence of a physical blow, I burst into a dazzling world of white, an Arctic panorama that whirled uncomprehendingly before my eyes. I looked down, and saw only blue! For long seconds I stared stupidly, thinking is this death? Then I looked up and saw – the ground! Terrifyingly close and spinning rapidly – the reaction came quickly. I was still alive, but only seconds away from the ground, in a steep spiral dive, over the vertical. Adrenalin thudded into my frozen limbs as I tried to roll the aircraft.

But now I had released the pull force and the speed was increasing; I could not move the ailerons! In desperation I got two hands on the stick, and slowly she responded. The ground leaped towards me as I pulled back on the control column, then I grazed the top of a mountain, and pulled out in a long sweeping dive in the valley beyond.

The speed fell, and I circled in the valley, my legs shaking uncontrollably, as I opened up to full power and started to climb. The aeroplane seemed to have survived the ordeal as I headed south looking for a pinpoint. I glanced over my shoulder at the thundercloud now looking malevolent and angry as though aware that its intended victim had escaped. I was more shaken than I had ever been in my life, and now I began to realise the series of stupid mistakes I had made.

I remembered as though it was a photograph, the vibrating instrument panel, and now I realised the significance of the turn indicator – of course, it had been showing a maximum rate turn!

I let the Tiger settle on the grass of the airfield, and taxied in. For the first time I was glad to get out of an aeroplane, and I knew that I had come to a crossroads, and that the next flight would be the significant one. But time is a great healer, especially when one is young, and although I still pushed my luck, as I suppose most youngsters do, it was never quite the same again.

I had pitted my skill against the elements, and lost! I would not be caught again, so I declared a halt in my unauthorised aerobatics while I learned how to fly a Tiger on instruments. This stood me in good stead on many occasions, but it was a long time before I ventured near another cumulus cloud!

Nowadays the tendency is to teach pilots enough to allow them to turn through 180 degrees and get out of trouble; but a little knowledge is possibly a dangerous thing. It might perhaps be better to insist that they stay out of cloud at all costs, at least until they have had a proper instrument course and have the necessary radio aids to be able to operate safely.

It is no good flying in or on top of cloud without navigation or communication, because you have to come down some time, and occasionally clouds have hard centres!

3

500 feet, 300 feet, now 200 feet, and still nothing.
This is crazy, I thought...

Where Angels
Fear to Tread

IN these days of closely regulated aviation, one is used to operating in accordance with the 'book' – the operations manual – with regard to company minima. Woe betide any pilot who descends below his decision height unless he has the required amount of runway or approach lights in sight. And should he so much as initiate an approach when the reported RVR is below his company limits, he will find himself on the carpet almost before his engines have stopped turning! In short, in these controlled times there is no place for pilot individuality, or initiative.

Not all pilots are the same; some are graced with more natural ability than others; yet others, through sheer effort, reach the same high standard. But airlines don't want a few brilliant pilots: they want a safe, responsible, standard team of pilots. So there may be an element of frustration amongst the more talented when they know they could land safely in bad weather, but have to divert because the 'book' says so.

At a time like this, all they can do is sigh, and think of their salary! But it was not always like this. Not so many years ago, pilots were encouraged to 'have a go', and while this may have been acceptable to the more skilled pilots, the result was, inevitably, that some of the others didn't quite make it – and 'didn't quite' was the epitaph of many a pilot, and his passengers, in those days.

There was always a point, somewhere, when every pilot reached his limit, and this varied from day to day, and often depended on how smoothly the initial approach had been flown.

On a few occasions the weather reports were so bad that there was no point in even setting out, so the decisions could be easily made. It was on such a day, some twelve years ago, that we sat around the crewroom, drinking the inevitable RAF coffee. The engineer, half frozen from his meticulous pre-flight inspection of the Hastings transport, burst into the room and made for the coffee bar.

'Take your time,' I said. 'We're not going anywhere yet.' The forecast at our destination was fog; most of the nearby civil airports were closed; I intended to wait a couple of hours, then look at the Met reports again.

The engineer had barely started his coffee when the door opened, and the Squadron Commander came in. Energetic and promotion-conscious, this was more than he could stand. 'Get airborne and try,' he said. 'You've got enough fuel to come back!'

Getting a big transport into the air is not a 5-minute job, but we were rolling down the runway in record time that morning – not a good start to the day. With the palm of my hand behind the throttles, number four engine leading, I slowly opened up to full power, letting the tail rise slowly of its own accord. Nobody takes any liberties with a Hastings. Indeed, every time a Hastings lands, everybody stops work to look: the results are very often quite spectacular!

At 8,000 feet we looked down on an even blanket of white cloud that covered the country as far as we could see. Beautiful it might be, but also perhaps lethal: the forecast had promised fog at our destination. I twisted round in my seat, and looked at the fuel gauges on the engineer's panel – we had plenty. Now it was time to contact approach control at our destination, and as we did so I was surprised to hear an aircraft calling downwind for ILS.

This should be interesting, I thought, as we listened to his progress around the circuit. We heard him call established, then declare his intention of carrying out a touch-and-go landing!

Either he's crazy, we thought, or he knows more about actual conditions on the approach than the Met forecaster does. As we cruised onwards, we listened with more than usual interest to his progress. In reply to his report at the outer marker, the tower cleared him to land, or roll.

Now we followed his descent using our spare VHF set. We could imagine him letting down into the fog: we knew how long it should take him, and we listened in silence, apart from the faint crackle of the R/T and the muted growl of our four Hercules radial engines. Suddenly the R/T sprang to life: he was on the runway, and rolling for another approach!

Now it was our turn to break in on the R/T. The radar controller turned us downwind, then read out the weather report – it was as bad as ever! Perplexed, we decided that it was probably the Met man, poring over his charts but failing to look out of his office window, who had not noticed a sudden clearance. Such things had been known before!

We were number two downwind to the unknown aircraft ahead: again he elected to carry out an ILS approach, but I opted for a GCA. This would give me a double check. I would fly the GCA, and monitor it with ILS, so that I could have two sets of continuous information; also, if one failed I could go straight on to the other.

We carried out the pre-landing check, and out of my side window I could see the giant mainwheel slowly easing itself out of the nacelle.

Flying a Hastings is a bit like commanding a ship: the co-pilot operates flaps and undercarriage, the engineer controls the throttles and rpm from his remote position, and also monitors fuel, temperatures and pressures, while the radio operator does the R/T. The navigator monitors the pilot's approach and identifies the approach aids. I had decided to use 200 feet as the height from which to overshoot if I still had not seen anything.

As the radar controller turned us on to a dog-leg for finals, I heard him tell the preceding aircraft to 'lock on' to the ILS, and call the tower for his touch-and-go. He acknowledged, and asked the controller to pass a message to his squadron to ask the next pilot to be prepared to change with him after the next approach, as 'conditions were good'.

This was good news to us, in spite of the persistent fog reports: if these people were doing continuation training, the weather must be all right. Now it was our turn. As we reached the glide-path, the co-pilot lowered full flap, and the engineer reduced power to -2lb boost. Now I would call for any power changes. If we overshot, the co-pilot would have to wind the trim forward as the power came on, because I would need all my strength with both hands on the wheel to control the tremendous trim change.

Though the Hastings was incredibly heavy to manoeuvre, it was easy to fly on instruments. The controller's voice droned monotonously on – 'You're on the centreline, on glide-path' – this was a good approach.

I watched the ILS zero reader out of the corner of my eye – it was dead centre and steady. Now we were in the grey murk, and with every passing instant I expected to see a change in colour beneath that would signify cloud base. But it remained cold, and wet, and grey.

'You are now number one,' said the controller – the other aircraft had made his touch-and-go. 500 feet, 300 feet, now 200 feet, and still nothing. This is crazy, I thought – the aircraft in front had said conditions were good. 150 feet – still nothing. 'I will continue talkdown,' said the controller. 'You're on centreline, on glide-path.' 100 feet, still the clinging grey blanket. Everyone was tense. I made my decision; I would overshoot, late, but not too late.

I flicked on my microphone to call the engineer for power, but as I did so I saw two lights, a white line directly below, and a white-painted figure 8 – I was above the runway with 8,000 feet to go! I called for a slow cut and drew the wheel back hard. The engine note died to a rumble and there was a squeal of rubber on concrete. We were down, with a smooth landing as well!

The airfield was shrouded in fog – we had broken out at only 75 feet above the runway!

The airfield was shrouded in fog – we had broken out at only 75 feet above the runway! What had gone wrong? I turned off the runway and stopped. The other aircraft was starting his final descent on the ILS. I would wait here and see what sort of an aircraft it was, and who were these ace pilots who considered these foul conditions 'good'.

With straining eyes we peered into the murk, until a grey shape emerged, running smoothly down the runway, engines idling. The lesson I learned that day has stayed with me ever since. Written in large letters along the fuselage of the Varsity was – 'Blind Landing Experimental Unit'!

4

Now it became a purposeful, shark-like creature, thrusting forwards and upwards – now it was coming into its element.

Mastering the Mosquito

THE Auster rattled and lurched as it made slow progress northwards into the teeth of a stiff breeze. As I looked out at the countryside stretching away before us, I reviewed the events of the past few days. A telephone call had started it all, and a familiar voice had asked, 'Have you flown a Mosquito?' Now, I knew very well that when that particular voice asks a question like that, there is usually some very interesting flying to follow. So while admitting that I hadn't actually flown one (I hadn't even seen inside one), I assured him that I had had plenty of twin-engined flying. Canberras and Meteors, it seemed, didn't qualify, but it so happened that I was then current on Dakotas. 'You shouldn't have any trouble then,' was the comment, and I was then informed that the initial task was to ferry a Mosquito Mk 35 from Liverpool to Bovingdon, where it was to take part in a film. It was also suggested that if I didn't break it in the process, I would be able to fly it in the film.

A phone call to the Board of Trade (as it was then) brought the first problem; it was apparently necessary to have a dual check and to sit the written examination on the type before flying it solo. Protests that there were no dual-controlled Mosquitoes left fell on stony ground. Once again the old RAF quip about Gibraltar came to mind.

I could see the only chance I was likely to have of flying a Mosquito slipping away, but I recalled that there was already a Mosquito at Bovingdon, which was being operated for the film company by a very experienced pilot, who was also a very old friend and who was an official examiner on type!

I drove over to Bovingdon and arrived just as Taffy was landing, watching his technique with more than passing interest as he carefully brought the machine in for a 'wheeler' landing. Obviously even he was taking no chances. I met him in dispersal with the suggestion that he should demonstrate a circuit, then swap seats to check me out, but while he was quite happy to demonstrate a circuit, he was adamant that he wouldn't ride on the observer's seat in a Mosquito with anybody! How, then, was I supposed to be checked out? He thought for a while, then came up with a suggestion – he would demonstrate a circuit, and I could get some taxiing practice after landing. He would then know nothing more until a second Mosquito appeared, undamaged, at Bovingdon. In the apparently unlikely event of this occurring, he would sign my Board of Trade form.

So ran my thoughts as the Auster crawled northwards, uncomfortably cramped in the noisy cockpit.

I landed at Liverpool, and there, majestic, powerful and gleaming in its camouflage paint, stood the Mosquito. I had thought that I would slip away with the minimum of fuss, but at this point fate took a hand. The machine belonged to the City of Liverpool and had been restored to take part in a film entitled *Mosquito Squadron*.

This had brought considerable publicity to the project and the whole airfield was alive with TV, radio and press reporters. Also, it needed a test flight as it hadn't flown for five years. I heard all this with a terrible sinking feeling.

'Have you any experience of flying Mosquitoes?' asked one reporter.

'Yes,' said I, thinking of my solitary circuit as a passenger the day before, and hoping he wouldn't ask any more revealing questions.

Finally the machine was ready for an air test. Not only was I committed to fly in front of a critical audience, but I also had to land the thing in front of TV cameras. No first solo student could have been more nervous. My crew member was the engineer responsible for the rebuild – at least he looked confident.

We settled into the tiny cockpit, bulky in our flying kit and parachutes. The engineer had to be very careful that he didn't accidentally touch the fuel cocks; it would have been only too easy to twist a little in his seat and turn off the fuel.

The view from the cockpit seemed to be almost completely obscured by propeller blades, and I observed uncomfortably that the arc of the propellers was in line with my legs.

With a whine the starter engaged on No 1 engine, and as the prop started to turn I pressed the booster coil button. The massive blades rebounded slightly with the gears banging and protesting, but at least I was familiar with the Merlin engine. I pulled the throttle back slightly and the engine immediately caught. No 2 started easily, and the view improved as the propellers blurred.

Running through the checks quickly because of the danger of overheating, I taxied towards the runway, thankful for the practice of the day before at Bovingdon.

My crew member had done a lot of flying in Mosquitoes, but I thought it prudent not to let on that he was about to become a passenger on a first solo, although I couldn't help noticing that he watched my every action like a hawk. Perhaps the fact that I had given him Pilot's Notes and asked him to read all checks aloud had something to do with it.

I ran the engines up to static rpm and checked CSU and mags; the Merlins thundered deafeningly while the aircraft shuddered and jerked against the brakes. Throttling back I noticed with concern the coolant bubbling acid boiling away from the vents on top of the engines. Although the radiator shutters were wide open, the temperature was rising rapidly – obviously there was no time to be lost; cooling air was necessary and the only way to get it was to fly.

I taxied onto the long runway and let the machine roll forward to straighten the tailwheel, which was non-castoring, and increased rpm to 1,500 against the brakes. The aircraft trembled urgently as though it was eager to be off. I released the brakes, and she started to roll forward. Carefully I used the brakes to keep exactly on the centreline; I remembered Taffy's advice – 'Open up slowly'!

As she gathered speed I used coarse rudder, but this was barely effective. Now, as she was running straight, was the moment to increase power; I twisted my wrist slightly so that I led fractionally with the left engine. The throttles were very highly geared so that the slightest error resulted in a large alteration of power with the attendant possibility of a swing, and a swing on take-off in a Mosquito is incipient disaster.

At 80 knots the tail came up and the throttles reached the gate. In the flying altitude she accelerated rapidly and now there was good rudder control, so I pulled the releases on the throttles and pushed them both fully forward. The noise was stupendous and my right foot was well forward to hold her straight, but now she was under control.

Slowly, very slowly, the gear came up...

At 105 knots I eased back on the stick and she lifted easily into the air, but we were not out of the wood yet. In the event of an engine failure I needed 185 knots (safety speed) to be sure of retaining control, and the speed had by now stabilised at 140 knots. What was wrong? I checked the instruments – both engines were developing maximum power – the strident roar of the Merlins was sweet and healthy. Two amber lights glaring at me gave the answer – undercarriage drag. Even those two magnificent engines at full power could only just hold the enormous drag of the undercarriage, and of course the flaps were still at the take-off setting, and the radiator shutters were open. The machine was trying to climb, but I forced it to remain in level flight – I needed speed, and those engines hadn't flown for five years – anything might be wrong, and if one of them failed… I put the thought out of my mind.

The hydraulic system on the Mosquito is practically the same as on the old Airspeed Oxford, but whereas the Oxford's undercarriage is quite neat and compact, the Mosquito's is massive by comparison. Slowly, very slowly, the gear came up, pulling the doors closed by a very Heath Robinson system of cables and rollers. As the main wheels locked up, the undercarriage lever sprang back into neutral, and again I had to change hands on the control column to reselect 'undercarriage up'. This was to make sure the tailwheel had retracted, and in fact this was immediately confirmed by the action of the lever again returning of its own accord to neutral.

Speed was now increasing, and I quickly selected flaps up and radiator shutters closed. Up to now the Mosquito had been struggling sluggishly, trying to rear up, but as it passed 200 knots its character began to change. Now it became a purposeful, shark-like creature, thrusting forwards and upwards – now it was coming into its element. I throttled back and reduced rpm to climbing power – still it accelerated, not perhaps as quickly as a Spitfire, but with steady determination. It felt solid, and yet eager to respond to the touch – one sensed its lethal potential as a war machine. Now it had surpassed the Spitfire's cruising speed, and still it accelerated. No wonder it was acclaimed as the fastest bomber of the war, relying on speed for safety, and therefore, in its initial concept, discarding the need for guns. It was light and sensitive on the ailerons, but strangely heavy and well damped in pitch. The rudder was extremely light, and hardly needed to be used at speed, and in this it was very like a jet aeroplane. Time was meaningless; the minutes sped like seconds, and all too soon it was time to go back.

The north coast of Wales flashed by at an incredible speed beneath us – what a contrast to the Auster! Banking at 80 degrees as we entered the free lane running down the estuary, the Mosquito was past the City of Liverpool in seconds as I throttled back to join the circuit. Revs up, rad shutters open, gear down, that incredibly slow travelling gear, and now increase power to offset the drag, flaps to 'take-off' and brakes checked.

We were still on main tanks, although we had 'proved' the outer tank flows in flight. I flew a long downwind leg and cautiously lined up with the runway; luckily, the wind was straight down it, and a beautiful 7,000 feet of concrete stretched ahead of us.

Remembering Taffy's advice, I kept the speed up and delayed selecting full flap until quite late – there was still time for an engine to fail. As the flaps went fully down I adjusted the throttles to allow the speed to reduce slowly. The note of the engines had subsided to a deep grumble, which blended with the hiss of the propellers. The view was excellent, I could see everything, perched as I was so far forward. Now concentrate, here comes the runway, start the flare slowly, and at the same time reduce power gently. As the revs fall, the aircraft

starts to sink and I pull back on the stick to control this. Down, down, and now there is concrete beneath the wheels, lower, lower, then the squeak of protesting rubber as the wheels touch at 100 knots. Now I press gently forward on the stick and slowly throttle fully back with the Merlins characteristically crackling and popping. Fully under control she runs straight, but remember what Taffy said – 'When the tail comes down she'll try to swing.'

I hold the tail up as long as possible where the rudder can bite into the clear air and give good control. At last the tail starts to drop, but I am ready. As the tailwheel touches down, stick fully back and brakes half on – now I steer with brakes, and as a complete anticlimax she rolls straight and true. Carefully I taxi into dispersal – the first hurdle is over. The engines slow and stop and silence lies heavily in the cockpit. I turn to the engineer.

'Well,' said I, 'that was a first solo.'

'I thought so,' he replied. 'Mosquitoes never swing on a first solo landing!'

5

Those who have heard the noise a Lancaster makes on take-off can have little idea of the noise levels in the cockpit with four Merlins at full blast.

Lancaster

LIKE a great white sea bird the Lancaster dominated the sky, her broad wings spanning over a hundred feet. Once a creature of the night, black and forbidding, now she was displayed in a white livery for only a few months earlier she had been in service with the French in New Caledonia in the maritime reconnaissance role.

Mere chance had prevented her from rotting away in a foreign clime, for she had been selected to retrace her path over half the world, to come home to England where she was to be preserved. And so, she turned her blunt nose to the north and her long journey began. Many were the problems she encountered, but she did not falter as she steadily ate up the miles, almost as if she knew she was going home. And finally, proudly, she made it. The airfield at Biggin Hill was alive with excitement, as with a deep throbbing beat from her four Merlins, the Lancaster settled onto the runway.

It was indeed a day for celebration, for tomorrow the work of restoring her as a civil aeroplane would begin. And as the work started it fell to Bill Fisher, who had initiated the project, to find a crew. It was at this point that I became involved with the project, because I was then a test pilot at the Royal Aircraft Establishment, Farnborough, where I was current on Shackletons. Bill knew that I had flown Hastings and Lincolns and so he asked me to find a crew for 'his Lancaster'.

In fact, finding a crew was no problem at all at Farnborough where most of the experienced 'four-engined' crews had at some time flown Lancasters. The big problem was that the aircraft only had eleven crew positions! Finally I chose three engineers and two navigators, the latter to allow me to forget any navigational problems so that I could really concentrate on the test programme.

I was a little concerned that I had had no Lancaster experience at all, whereas Charlie, one of the engineers, had about 3,000 hours on type! But at least I was in good hands engineering-wise.

Finally the great day dawned and she stood there transformed. No longer wearing her white tropical garb, now she was once again in the dull black and camouflage of RAF Bomber Command of World War 2. Now she looked purposeful and powerful – and precious, for she was the only airworthy Lancaster. The engine runs had been carried out and she had been declared serviceable – now it was up to us.

The drills which we went through everyday on the Shackleton at Farnborough now stood us in good stead, for starting a Lancaster is really a four-handed job. The engineer looks after the fuel system, radiator shutter, booster coil and starter buttons, while the pilot operates the master cocks, throttles and switches. An athletic groundcrewman has to climb up onto the main wheels, a tricky business when the inboard engines are running, in order to prime the two engines on that side. During this operation it is only too easy for the pilot to allow an engine to stop in his efforts to coax its neighbour into life. This incurs the wrath of the ground engineer, who is now leaping on and off the main wheels like a demented goat.

Eventually with all engines running one can embark upon an exercise which can almost reduce strong men to tears; I refer to taxying a four-engined piston tailwheel aeroplane, with pneumatic brakes of monumental hysteresis and dubious efficiency! The technique of taxying a Lancaster is to keep the inboard engines at 800rpm to stop them oiling up, and to allow No.3 to preserve a modicum of brake pressure whilst the outboards are used in great bursts of power to steer the aeroplanes. One tries at all times to conserve precious braking power.

At first there is a tendency to weave a drunken path down the peri-track with the outboards alternately going from high boost to slow running, the aeroplane gathering speed all the while, until the situation either gets completely out of control, or one gives up, throttles back all four, and expends brake pressure in attempting to stop 40,000lbs of careering aeroplane.

If the latter exercise is successful, one breathes a sigh of relief while running No.3 at 1,500rpm to restore brake pressure, which invariably infuriates air traffic control as all taxying traffic grinds to a halt. It also allows the pilot to sort out what went wrong that time!

Take-off, by contrast, is quite straight forward. The engines are opened up to zero boost and the brakes are released. As the aeroplane starts to move forward I lead with No.1 throttle to keep straight. I let the tail lift on its own and as the rudders become effective I release the throttles and ask the engineer for full power.

Those who have heard the noise a Lancaster makes on take-off can have little idea of the noise levels in the cockpit with four Merlins at full blast. The noise is indescribable but unlike jet engines at high power the song of four Merlins at plus 14lbs boost and 3,000rpm gives a much greater feeling of power, and the acceleration of such a big aircraft is most impressive.

Once the gear and flaps are up the aircraft is really in its element, so much so that our engineer remarked that comparing the Lancaster with a Shackleton was akin to comparing a greyhound with an elephant.

On that first flight she performed like a real lady, and we were all agreed that she was a gentle and docile aeroplane. But we had yet to see her teeth, and we didn't have long to wait.

On the next flight I had to feather and un-feather each engine in turn, No.1 performed OK and now it was the turn of No.2. I watched the spinner slowing down as the engineer pressed the feathering button but instead of stopping it started to accelerate again, gradually at first, but then with alarming rapidity. I had never seen this happen before, but I knew all too well what was about to occur.

I just had time to shout 'Runaway Prop' before all communication was swamped by an ear-splitting blare of sound that stunned the mind with its awesome ferocity. I pulled the nose up as quickly as I dared to kill the airspeed, because that was the source of the terrible energy being absorbed by the propeller. As I did, I saw the rpm rising from 3,200; the engineer later told me that it reached at least 3,600. He was very fast off the mark and had turned off fuel and switches and was trying by means of the pitch lever and feathering button to slow the racing propeller down.

I was reluctant to throttle back the remaining engines too fast or too far in case they too oversped. Even at reduced power on three engines, the Lancaster was climbing fast, so I selected wheels and flaps down – I needed high drag and quickly.

In the pushover we entered cloud just as the artificial horizon toppled, and the airspeed hovered around the 100 knots mark. But now three engines were back at -2lbs boost and the runaway had stabilised at 2,400rpm. There was no radio or intercom as this had failed when the engine oversped. The engineer had also seen the fire warning light illuminate, and had hit the extinguisher – which of course didn't work!

Gradually order was restored and some practical engineering under the navigator's table produced intercom and enough radio to make a distress call.

We worked at the port inner, spinning away merrily at 2,400rpm and decided not to fool about with it any more. All pressures and temperatures were OK so I thought I would let sleeping dogs lie – that thing was spinning too close to my seat for comfort. The ensuing three-engined landing caused a fair amount of excitement on the ground but was a complete anti-climax after what we had just been through.

Luckily we had saved the engine and were able to go on and finish the test programme. There was more excitement to come before we did, but that is another story.

At last we flew her to the No.617 Squadron reunion on the 24th. anniversary of the Dams raid, and we flew over the bomber airfields of Lincolnshire, and over Waddington where we looked down on PA474, the RAF's Lancaster doomed at that time to static exhibition, before going on to Scampton.

Now the boot is on the other foot and it is NX611 which guards the gates at Scampton, while 474 fills the sky with her thunder and reminds us of those dark brave days of World War 2 when she and her kind carried the hopes of us all. We like to think that our flight that day was instrumental in getting the RAF's Lanc back into the air. Long may she remain airworthy - now in reality, the last of the many.

6

I coasted over the top of the loop in deathly silence,
feverishly juggling with fuel cock and throttle, having
only achieved 350 metres above the ground. With all
the intensity of youth I pressed on...

Ballerina

By the late 1930s racing aircraft in the USA were beginning to achieve frightening speeds. With the trend to ever smaller airframes and bigger engines, they were becoming less stable and controllable. As their engines were tuned to the absolute peak of performance, they sometimes failed, often with drastic results. Where all this would have ended one may only guess, because the Second World War put a stop to it all for six years.

When the air races were held again after the war the older generation of racers had gone, but had been replaced by ex-military fighter aircraft able to achieve unheard-of speeds. But with these high speeds came also a tragic toll of accidents. In 1947, in an attempt to restore an element of sanity to air racing, the Goodyear Trophy formula for racers was evolved. The specification demanded stock engines with a displacement of 190 cubic inches or less, and there were also defined minimum limits for wing area, stalling speed, type of landing gear, and propellers. The formula was immediately popular, for not only could the average man in the street identify with these tiny home-built aeroplanes, but during their races round close-set pylons they remained in view the whole time, looking and sounding like a swarm of angry hornets. The art of the designer was to place the most streamlined frame possible around these tiny engines, and to concentrate on surface finish and especially propeller design.

But not all of these machines were home-built. Tony Le Vier, a Lockheed test pilot who also had considerable experience of racing in the Unlimited category, formed an association to construct a Formula One racer, as they had come to be known, and in the first Goodyear Trophy of 1947 he won third place with his Cosmic Wind 'Minnow', flown by fellow test pilot 'Fish' Salmon. In the same race the following year, Salmon, flying a much-modified 'Minnow', achieved first place. By this time there were no fewer than three Cosmic Winds – 'Minnow', 'Little Toni' and 'Ballerina' – and these three came to be known as the 'terrible triplets'.

After the resurgence of air racing in the UK after the war, 'Ballerina' found its way across the Atlantic. It was bought for the Tiger Club, and here it made history, for not only did it become a club aircraft, albeit restricted to the club's best pilots, but it also became the pride of the Tiger Club displays. It still raced, though only in handicap races, and in the hands of the Redhill racing pilots it added to its already impressive list of victories.

Not only was 'Ballerina' the first Cosmic Wind in Britain (and now there are two more), but it was the first, and probably the last, Formula One racer ever to compete in the World Aerobatic Championships. When we first flew it we were all highly impressed by its incredible handling by comparison with our Stampe biplanes. 'Ballerina' had a roll rate of 360 degrees per second and enormous strength. Of course it had no inverted fuel or oil system, but that didn't deter the display pilots. It had a maximum diving speed of 300mph, and handled more like a miniature Hunter than a piston-engined aeroplane. It could fly eight-point vertical rolls, although the engine was nominally only 85hp; but perhaps the most spectacular manoeuvre during this period was a dead-stick outside loop, which was our favourite way of starting a display. Indeed, we expanded on this, pulling up from 240mph and flying a half inside loop, followed by an upward outside loop with no power available. The 'g' forces were very wearing after the docile old Stampes, and the noise the machine made at high speed was quite deafening, as there was little room for a helmet inside the tiny canopy.

The cockpit itself was deceptively large, so that a 14-stone 6-foot pilot still had plenty of elbow room, although getting in and out might be a bit of a struggle. With one's shoulders wedged under the metal canopy surround one felt curiously secure, even before the straps were tightened, and indeed it was very handy to be able to use the sides of the cockpit to stabilise one's body laterally against the incredible rate of roll. One sat very low to the ground, it seemed, and this sensation was accentuated by the fact that one's legs were nearly horizontal, a situation that markedly increased the tolerance of the pilot to both positive and negative 'g'.

The safety harness consisted of a broad lap belt with leather thigh pads, on to which was clipped the shoulder harness. It gave one considerable cause for thought to realise that there was no negative 'g' strap or back-up harness, so that any failure of the main harness in inverted flight would catapult the pilot straight out of the aeroplane, canopy or no. To be sure, there was a rather ancient back-type parachute, but I would not have bet on its

operational effectiveness. Another interesting point about the shoulder harness was a modification that was incorporated in the event of a crash-landing, in which piano wire was sewn along the centre of the strap and attached to the buckle, the other end being secured to the fuselage aft of the seat. When the straps were pulled tight, this thin wire slackened off, and it did not take much imagination to visualise the result of a sudden deceleration – ever seen a grocer cutting cheese with a similar piece of wire? Needless to say, this modification was quickly removed!

'Ballerina' on take-off, unless the surface was glassy smooth, was a law unto herself. With only 4 inches of propeller clearance in the flying attitude, one dare not raise the tail too high, with the result that she bounded enthusiastically across the grass with the pilot unable to do anything except hang on grimly and hope for the best. Sometimes, just to add to the pilot's discomfiture, the engine would cut out, or run irregularly: this could occasionally be cured by throttling back, then opening up again. On a rough surface the best one could hope for was to survive long enough for the speed to reach about 75mph, whereupon 'Ballerina' could be persuaded to leave the ground.

It was then a matter of being patient while she slowly accelerated beyond her minimum drag speed of about 90mph. Then things really started to happen! Like a frisky colt she would decide that speed was the thing: if one held her down she would be doing nearly 170mph by the end of the runway, at which point she positively demanded that an aerobatic manoeuvre be carried out. This sort of waywardness got many a pilot into trouble for unauthorised low-level aerobatics, for anyone who had not flown 'Ballerina' could never know the irresistible temptation to use the performance afforded by those incredible ailerons. Beautifully balanced, they were almost full span, light but strong, and equipped with two aerodynamic/mass balances on each side, these being flush with the underside of the wing with the stick neutral. They gave 'Ballerina' her superb handling in roll: there was never any sign of adverse aileron yaw, and rolls could be started and stopped almost instantaneously.

As a handling aeroplane she approached perfection, though in terms of pure speed she was not up to expectations. Above 170mph acceleration dropped off rapidly, and in her earlier days she had never been able to match the speeds of some of the other Formula One racers. To be fair, it is doubtful if any of them could have equalled the marvellous control response and harmonisation of the Cosmic Winds. It seemed that good handling qualities and exceptional speed did not go hand in hand, at least as far as the midget racers were concerned. 'Ballerina' was best flown by mere pressures on the stick. A racing turn needed scarcely more than the thought – the pilot merely leaned into the turn and she was round and away. If she had any faults, they were overshadowed by her virtues. At very high speed, with the controls iron-hard and the slipstream roaring furiously outside the tiny canopy, the aircraft would try to snake from side to side. It was dangerous to try to correct it; one could merely clamp one's feet hard on the rudder pedals. The elevator had to be used with extreme care at speed, for the stick force per 'g' was quite low.

She did have disadvantages from an aerobatic point of view: she was too fast, and would flash from one end of the box to the other almost faster than her pilot could cope with; and she had no inverted system. This latter problem was thought easy to solve, so a rather primitive fuel system was devised that allowed fuel to reach the carburettor regardless of attitude, and which embodied an extension to the jet. Looking at the drawings again, I cannot imagine how it ran at all.

The biggest problem was that in certain attitudes the mixture became too rich and the engine stopped, so the pilot had to anticipate this problem and select fuel 'off' momentarily to avoid a cut. It shows the attitude of near-desperation in which we competed in those days, since I had to turn the fuel off sixteen times during one free sequence in order to keep the engine running.

Another small problem we encountered during the 1964 championships was that the maximum height permitted in the known compulsory sequence was only 500 metres, the minimum height being 100 metres. It so happened that the outside looping diameter of 'Ballerina' was 400 metres, so it will be seen that the sequence was only just possible if the engine kept running, and inevitably, in the first round of the World Championship, it stopped as I was entering the outside loop! I coasted over the top of the loop in deathly silence, feverishly juggling with fuel cock and throttle, having only achieved 350 metres above the ground. With all the intensity of youth I pressed on until I was diving vertically, but still the engine remained silent. At last common sense prevailed and I pulled out to complete a dead-stick landing in front of the judges, who were apparently so relieved that they let me have another attempt at the sequence!

There were some advantages to flying such a strange machine in the contest, not the least of which was the fact that nobody knew what manoeuvres such as flick-rolls were supposed to look like. During the unknown compulsory programme, which included several manoeuvres I had not flown before, I was demoralised to watch world-famous pilots falling out of control from them. One such figure was an inverted flick-roll with an inverted climb of 45 degrees. I determined to use the novelty of 'Ballerina' to my advantage: at the appropriate moment I gave the rudder a nudge, pushed forward a little on the stick, and slammed on full aileron. In a flash she was around the roll, and still hurtling upwards at 45 degrees. I would not have dared to flick-roll at that speed! It was one of the very few times that I achieved the maximum score of ten points – and I had not even stalled the aircraft!

But still, trickery apart, she was not ideally suited. Because she was so small (only 19½ feet span) she had to be flown at low level to be seen at all, and with only 85hp she soon ran out of speed. The box, 1,000 metres long, was not sufficiently large for her to accelerate again, and it was this that really lost the marks. Still, she was the sensation of the competition, and resulted in the US team considering entering a small but very powerful aeroplane, such as the Pitts Special. Even the Czechs constructed a small machine with a Walter engine called the 'Racek' ('Seagull'), but this came to nothing.

Several pilots from foreign teams flew 'Ballerina' and were astonished at what could be achieved on 85hp. One pilot wound her up to 250mph, rolled inverted (whereupon the engine cut out), and pushed, hoping to achieve an outside loop. All that was needed with 'Ballerina' was a light stick pressure: before he knew what had happened he had pushed seven negative 'g'! When he got down, the whites of his eyes had turned – literally – blood red! Even the Russians tried her for size: the briefing, via interpreter, was quite hilarious, but reached its peak when the function of the mixture control was described. There was a discourse in Russian, then a beam of enlightenment spread across the Soviet pilot's face. 'Ah!' he said, 'Smersh!' – apparently the Russian word for 'mixture', but with a different meaning for us James Bond fans.

The performance of 'Ballerina' was due in part to a curiously ground McCauley metal propeller, shaped like a scimitar, and with almost parallel chord blades. We were given to understand that as the load came onto the propeller it fined off, giving good take-off and climb performance; but as speed increased, it reverted to its coarse setting. Although incredible zoom climb rates could be achieved, 'Ballerina' could only achieve about 1,200ft/min at 130mph, and one had to constantly remind oneself that it was only a 190-cubic-inch engine, such was the overall level of performance.

Certainly she did not like 1,000-foot circuits; the best way of arriving was to fly a scaled-down version of a jet fighter circuit, resulting in a height of about 300 feet downwind. This was a good way of keeping the speed from getting out of hand on finals, though it didn't tend to make 'Ballerina' or her pilots over-popular with ATC. By contemporary standards she was a slippery aeroplane; 85mph was the threshold speed, and an extra 5mph or so could add half a mile to the landing run. But she was sufficiently docile to accept low speed against power on the wrong side of the drag curve, when precision landings were possible.

When the engine stopped, which was frequently, one had to be exactly right, but I found that a steep sideslip was quite safe until the airflow could be heard to detach around the canopy – that was the time to kick her straight. On the landing roll one concentrated on holding the three-point attitude (never try a wheel landing with a 4-inch prop clearance) and on keeping wings level and nose pointed along the runway. She was meant to land on smooth tarmac, with the result that if one operated off grass she tended to bounce and porpoise in an alarming manner on her spring steel undercarriage. Also she had a sharp-edged lateral waddle that often gave the pilot a rap across the ear from the canopy. This sort of performance earned for her the nickname 'La Ranita', which in Spanish means 'Little Frog', on account of her being small and green, to say nothing of her ricocheting progress.

She came home from the World Championships covered in glory, but never competed again in an aerobatic competition. Then one day she was gone, tragically, off a tight turn at low altitude in an air race. Even at the end she let her pilot live, and she in turn refused to die, for today she flies again, rebuilt better than ever, as 'Ballerina II'. No longer is she an aerobatic contender; today she is cleaner and more streamlined and faster than ever before; her destiny now lies around the pylons of the Formula One race circuit.

7

...we were enthralled by a dazzling display of Northern Lights, dancing, shimmering, bursting, fading...

7,000-Mile Hoax

As a freelance pilot, the sort of work I find myself doing is varied and interesting, and covers a wide field of aviation, from air show flying, film work, ferry flying and air taxi operation. During the winter months the air taxi phase is the most predominant, so I consider myself fortunate that the aircraft I fly is not a common-or-garden light twin, but an expensive and sleek executive jet.

The Fanjet Falcon is really the Rolls-Royce of the air taxi world, and there is but a single specimen on the UK register of civil aircraft, based at Heathrow. Since the aircraft is operated under an AOC it follows that the crews are required to fly under very similar requirements to those of the state airlines, for example in the number of duty hours they may work in a day.

This system was introduced as a flight safety measure in days gone by when the world abounded in unscrupulous airline operators who would work their long-suffering aircrew in the most appalling manner, constituting not only a flight safety hazard but giving rise to stories in the popular press of pilots falling asleep at the controls!

Nowadays that sort of situation is a thing of the past, and the company for which I fly takes a pride in running itself efficiently and always within the laid-down legal requirements.

But those bad old days are not so far behind us that they are conveniently forgotten in the dim recesses of memory. It is but three short years since I worked for a different company, based in England and flying Falcons that were registered in France.

Because it was a French aircraft, the UK authorities felt no commitment to interfere, nor indeed did they have the right to do so. The French, because we were based in England, left us alone. We flew with a French validation on our UK licences, and there was no such thing as 'minimum duty hours'. We were pushed into doing flights that we would like to have refused, but to do so would mean losing our jobs, and jobs were hard to find.

We would find ourselves taking flights from other UK operators, because they were constrained by law from doing them, and we were not. True, we had a longer range than the HS125s, but we certainly never arrived with the reserve fuel required under UK regulations, especially on long flights. It was sometimes reminiscent of the so-called 'good old days' in Fighter Command, where we would taxi in with the low level warning fuel light on. We survived because we had experience and skill, and we gained experience with every flight.

Christmas and New Year were bad times for us, because our wealthy clients wanted to travel around Europe at all hours of the day or night. Christmas cheer was not for us, and we talked wistfully of those other years when we had been able to relax at home and watch our children playing with their Christmas toys. Now, our Christmas cheer consisted of seeing how many languages we could count wishing us a Merry Christmas as we laid condensation trails over the night skies of Europe.

It was hardly surprising, then, that when the operations manager rang up and said, 'You're taking off in 2 hours for Los Angeles,' my first thought was that it was a leg-pull, and my second thought was that he had cracked up! It would mean a flight time of 20 hours, and seven refuelling stops, a total of 35 hours on duty, and it was already six o'clock in the evening.

I had been up since eight that morning, so that would mean 43 hours without sleep, and no navigation aids except short-range airline equipment, such as VOR and ADF, with which to cross the north Atlantic in the depth of winter!

Now, these flights are all very well if you can plan them properly and you can wait for the weather, if necessary, but this was to be an ambulance flight, non-stop as far as possible, with a stretcher case all the way!

This was no leg-pull! I had a French co-pilot, who was just as tired as I was, both of us recovering from our previous marathon trip. Because of the distance, another pilot was appointed to the crew, an experienced French Falcon captain. There was no time for proper planning: we booked the weather forecast for the first leg to Iceland, and grabbed all the charts we could find. Driving through the teeming rain, I reached the terminal at Gatwick as the ambulance drew up. The flight plan was filed and we gently eased the stretcher into the aircraft. The patient was the wife of a famous film star who was 'seriously ill' – with what we were not told. Her film star husband accompanied her, and was obviously distraught.

Our other two passengers were a medical officer, just retired from the army, and a secretary. I had asked for Arctic survival gear, but there was none on board. 'You can pick it up in Iceland – we've requested it,' said the managing director.

I had suffered from his organisation before, but at this stage, with the passengers on board, there was not much I could do. The co-pilot and I clambered into the flight deck, while the French captain settled down on the jump seat to plan the next legs.

The runway lights faded into the murk ahead of me as I released the brakes and we started to roll on the first leg of our 7,000-mile mercy mission.

Soon the bustle and near panic of the preparations were forgotten as we broke out of cloud to be greeted by a star-studded sky of breathtaking brilliance, and for a few moments we remembered that it was Christmas, the season of joy, peace and goodwill. Then the controller's voice, clearing us to continue the climb, brought us back to reality. The workload was light, the controller monitoring us on radar, as we trekked from beacon to beacon, northwards, upwards. Soon we would swing to the north-west, to Iceland.

I was concerned about the patient – she had looked so white when we carried her on board. Now Scotland was behind us and we cruised out over the North Atlantic; soon the VOR signals began to fade and the needles fluctuated. Now it was back to basics; we steered a dead reckoning course – we had no sextant on board. Soon there was only one navigation aid left – Consol.

Originally used by vessels, including submarines, it was archaic in its presentation. I had learned it in flight school, but had never imagined that I would actually use it. A series of dots and dashes, numbering sixty in all, one had to count them and extrapolate if the number fell short of sixty. Then, by referring to a chart, one could draw a position line. By repeating this procedure with another station, one obtained a two-position line fix. Leaving the autopilot to fly the aircraft, I took fix after fix: I could not afford a mistake here. I double-checked ground speed and track by depressing the radar antenna fully and turning up the gain. This effectively destroyed the picture, but it did produce a series of lines caused by surface reflection, and by bisecting these lines on the scope I could assess drift. Then I turned down the gain and searched for a ship to give me a ground speed check.

The time passed quickly and before long we could pick up the beacon at Keflavik, double-checked by the radar scanner. We broke cloud at 2,000 feet with the airport lights seen through a film of water that almost defied the efforts of the windscreen wipers. The aircraft bucked and bounced – the surface wind was 50 knots! Conscious all the time of our passengers, I picked my moment and slid the aircraft onto the runway. Leaving our passengers on board in relative warmth, we made our way to the tower, heads bent against the screaming wind and lashing rain.

Sondestrom, in Greenland, for once promised good weather, and the headwind was not too strong at height. We arrived back at the aircraft to find not only that refuelling was completed but that the survival gear had arrived and had been stowed. Perhaps I had misjudged the managing director. With relief we heard the door close, blotting out the thunder of wind and rain.

Heavy with fuel, we lifted into the air, pounded by the merciless turbulence. I kept the airspeed low to minimise the effects on aircraft and occupants, and flew on instruments, even the blackness outside blotted out by the ice that formed on the semi-heated centre windscreen. Long minutes passed until again we soared high above the storm clouds, levelling at 39,000 feet.

As the lights faded for the last time we tried to use the H/F radio, through a crashing, crackling cacophony of static.

Now, with the windscreen clear again, we were enthralled by a dazzling display of Northern Lights, dancing, shimmering, bursting, fading, with colours indescribable. Like a curtain of silk, or bursting fireworks, sometimes a tremulous glow, then rising to a cascading waterfall of light from high above us, we were held spellbound by the sight. We stared and stared, almost hypnotised by the awesome beauty of the spectacle, and dragged our gaze away only to see that the navigation systems had unlocked, and we had lost voice communication with the outside world. We guessed that the incredible display of Northern Lights was responsible, in an eerie way, for they must be magnetic in their source.

As the lights faded for the last time we tried to use the H/F radio, through a crashing, crackling cacophony of static. But in the end it was the radar that showed the coast of Greenland. Tuning carefully, we soon produced a sharp image and were able to get a fix, and before long we were in VHF contact with the American radar controller. As we turned on finals we were surprised to learn that we were still 30 miles out! So clear was the light that it seemed the field was only 5 miles away, and we seemed to hang motionless in space. Now we understood why GCA is mandatory at Sondestrom, because it is impossible to judge distance. It is perhaps easier to land there when the visibility is bad – at least distances look normal then.

The final approach seemed never-ending, but by flying on instruments I was able to bring an air of reality to the proceedings. Greenland – what a name to give to this white hell! Though it was still night, the starlight reflected off the snow to illuminate the airfield with its soft, cold, light. The air stung the nose and lungs, but there was no wind, for which we were thankful.

It was 10 degrees below zero yet the air was so dry that it was bearable. Awed by the foreign landscape, we wondered how those early Danish settlers felt, lured to this place by the lush-sounding name – Greenland.

Now it was my turn in the right-hand seat, the co-pilot trying to sleep in the forward luggage bay as the French pilot pointed the nose upwards for our next leg to Goose Bay. I knew Goose – I had been there before, but never in winter.

Now we were coming back into civilisation, but with the ocean station off the air we could only guess our position. Still in darkness – would this night never end? – we started our descent, the voice of the Canadian controller confident in our earphones. I knew the standard of GCA in Canada was high, for I had trained there on jets. As we crept lower, the reasons for the high standards became apparent. Blowing snow, almost zero visibility, strong gusting winds, and we were very tired by now.

We would have to stop here for a few hours. I used every argument I knew to have our patient transferred to the military hospital for a time, but in the end it was only by using the medical officer's rank of colonel that I was successful.

We used the landing lights on finals only to hurriedly switch them off as the blinding reflection bounced off the wall of snowflakes in front of us. Braking, slithering, skidding on the hard-packed snow, we cautiously felt our way to the apron. A heated ambulance was there, engine running, ready for the transfer.

We shut down, and I told the crew to put on survival gear before going outside; I had lived in Canada in winter before. The co-pilot, enthusiastic, opened the door and jumped out, clad only in his uniform. He was outside for all of 2 seconds before he hurtled back in, teeth chattering, fingers burning with cold. It was 33 degrees below zero in a 30-knot wind – that made the temperature in wind chill equal to 60 degrees below zero!

We slammed the door and opened the survival kit – it was army surplus gear, full of holes, zips broken, buttons missing! There were no gloves. How we cursed our management; how we wished they had to endure that terrible cold without adequate protection! Somehow we transferred our passenger to the ambulance. Somehow we refuelled the aircraft – with the APU running all the time to stop everything from freezing solid.

We had a hot meal in the mess and grabbed 4 hours' sleep in the centrally heated dormitory. Now for the first time on this flight, we were in daylight. And what daylight! The snowstorm had vanished as quickly as it had come, and with it the wind. The sun shone down from a brilliant blue sky, but seemed to give no heat, in spite of its glare, amplified as it was by the dazzling snow. Muffled in our scarecrow survival gear, our boots squeaking on the snow, we set about opening the aircraft.

Keys refusing to penetrate frozen locks, hatches iced up solidly, it took 2 hours to prepare the aircraft for flight. Then we had all our problems of yesterday in reverse as we struggled and slipped in the snow and ice to transfer the stretcher with our patient from the heated ambulance to the Falcon.

At last all was ready, and we climbed into an azure sky, with unlimited visibility. But now we hit headwinds, and could not reach Ottawa. We landed instead at Dorval Airport, Montreal, and were surprised at the lavish General Aviation Terminal. Montreal was so efficient that we were in the air again within half an hour, bound for Kansas City, but again we were thwarted by headwinds, and landed instead at St Louis.

Here, for the first time, we ran into administrative problems. Because of our hurried departure we had not received visas for the USA, and this was to have been arranged at Kansas City. The local authorities at St Louis were reluctant to clear us outbound to the USA in case of repercussions – reluctant, that is, until it was realised whom we were carrying. I had not previously appreciated the power of Hollywood in the New World!

A flurry of autographs, a quick handshake, and we were on our way once more. Soon darkness overtook us again on the second day of our voyage, and with darkness came the desire to sleep. Airways flying in the USA is very restful: there is no need to report position, as watchful radar operators follow every move. Silence reigns on the darkened flight deck, the only sounds being the distant hum of the engines and the hiss of air around the windscreen. Before long I was the only one still awake, and even then I am sure I dozed for a few moments. As we later ruefully recalled, the only ones awake in the aircraft were George and Arthur, our code names for the automatic pilot and the artificial feel unit! At last the controller's voice roused us from our stupor, and we slid into the denser layers of the lower atmosphere.

Here we landed on the desert plateau airfield of Albuquerque where, in spite of the latitude, the night wind cut into our bones, recalling with a shiver the bleakness of Greenland. By now fatigue was affecting each member of the party and the film star was particularly distraught as his wife seemed to be weakening. Only one more leg, I thought, wondering whether I ought perhaps to insist that our patient should rest again before continuing. But the transfer from aircraft to hospital would be more tiring for her than the flight, so at the doctor's suggestion we decided to continue.

By now we had our second wind, and as the lights of Hollywood stretched before us, we felt relatively fresh. But this was short-lived, for as we rolled to a halt at Burbank, and shut down the engines at the end of our epic flight, we realised what a strain we had been under. Exhausted now, we slumped in our seats. Outside, a large black Cadillac drew up, awaiting our passengers. We heard the main door open with a thump, but before we could rouse ourselves, the sick lady, who had seemed on the point of quitting this world, jumped off her stretcher, leaned into the cockpit, thrust a piece of paper into my hand and said, 'Gee, boys, thanks for the ride!', whereupon she skipped down the steps, leaped into the waiting Cadillac, and was gone!

Thunderstruck, we stared at each other. It was the first time I ever saw a Frenchman at a loss for words. I looked at the piece of paper in my hand: it was a cheque of 25,000 dollars, the cost of our mercy mission! Was it a miracle cure we had witnessed – or was it a very expensive hoax? I never found out – and I hope the film star never did either!

8

It came without further warning, a giant hammer blow that caused the whole machine to shudder; the throttle kicked in my hand and now there really was vibration.

Things that Go Bang in Flight

AN airshow in Ireland is quite a rare event, but with the promise of real Irish hospitality and the relaxing atmosphere of a private airstrip in the heart of rolling green hills, we were only too happy to accept the offer. The Irish people were warm, friendly and generous to a fault, and our stay there was far too short. The display itself was a restful interlude amongst the hectic programme planned for us, dinner parties, sightseeing and innumerable invitations to visit our new acquaintances at their homes.

Of the display, little can be said; public and pilots alike had the time of their lives, and such was the wide-eyed charm of the local children that even some of our more crusty members melted and took time out to explain the intricacies of our strange assortment of flying machines.

All too soon it was over, and reluctantly we packed our gear for the last time. The local Customs officer came out to clear us direct to the mainland and, with the party atmosphere still going strong, by the time we finally got airborne he was beginning to view the scene through a slightly alcoholic haze. Indeed, some of our members had suggested that perhaps the weather would be better tomorrow; there was a forecast of poor visibility over the Irish Sea, and anyway there were still gallons of Irish beer yet to be consumed!

But we did eventually all get airborne, and all sober, which was no mean achievement in itself. I was in charge of navigation, and I was also flying the slowest aeroplane, a Stampe. We roared low over the display site in salute, then opened out into loose formation for the trip down the coast to our departure point; the lighthouse guarding St George's Channel.

The other machines were a motley collection: a racing Tiger Moth, an elderly Auster, and a Zlin. The countryside flowed past beneath, lush and rich, a bright green – no wonder it is called the Emerald Isle. The sun shone, the engines were pulling steadily, and life was good.

Soon the turning point came into view, and we slowly swung onto our new course, which was to take us out to sea, and eastwards towards home. Over the sea the visibility reduced in haze, and I dropped lower and lower; there is no artificial horizon in the Stampe, and I had to fly steadily with the other aircraft in formation on me. I had also to be accurate in my track-keeping, for none of the others were able to do any navigation for themselves and fly formation at the same time.

The visibility became worse, and we sank lower, still lower, using the surface of the sea to indicate lateral level – but not too low. That sea was smooth and glassy and it would be only too easy to fly into it. I concentrated hard, estimating the drift by eye. In fact, there wasn't much – the wind was light.

I felt the weight of responsibility heavily upon me. I must not make even the slightest mistake; everyone was relying on my judgement and calculations.

The journey seemed never-ending, although in reality the crossing was quite a short distance. All around was water, as far as the eye could see, and our progress over the smooth glassy surface became distorted; now it seemed we were rushing headlong into a translucent wall of haze, and at other times hanging motionless in space.

The second hand on the stopwatch marched rhythmically round the dial, counting off the miles; now, with only a few minutes to go to landfall, I peered into the haze, but there was nothing, only the sea.

As I stared through the windscreen it seemed that the haze was darker; it could mean only one thing. I signalled increased power and eased into a shallow climb, the other aircraft straggling out behind me, as the dark mass of the Welsh coast loomed out of the murk.

How different in character from the green island behind us. Here the black crags soared majestically out of the dark sea, the sea birds, startled by our arrival, wheeling in wide spirals at the face of the cliffs. At the summit the heather and mountain grass struggled for survival, for in bad weather this part of Wales meets the full force of the Atlantic gales.

But to me, if not to the others, this was home, and on track into the bargain, so I was well content as I levelled off at 1,500 feet on the last leg to the Customs airport at Swansea. With the haze of the sea crossing behind us I was able to drink in the scenery, so widely varied, from the coast on my right through the cultivated fields to the rolling hills in the north.

It seemed that even the aeroplane was reluctant to finish this magic journey, for we were flying noticeably more slowly, and the revs were down a little. Was it my imagination, or could I detect some vibration?

Normally one can persuade oneself that one can hear all manner of strange noises when over the water in a single-engined aeroplane, but on the sea crossing she had been as smooth as silk. 'Imagination,' I thought to myself, and opened the throttle a little, perhaps not yet fully convinced.

The harder I listened to the engine, the more I became certain that something was amiss, but I could not be absolutely certain. I throttled back again, determined that it could not be anything significant, and that I would have a good look around the aeroplane at Swansea. Soon we would be approaching the village where I had grown up, and I started to look for familiar landmarks; how small it all seemed coming back to it after all these years.

It came without further warning, a giant hammer blow that caused the whole machine to shudder; the throttle kicked in my hand, and now there really was vibration. I could hardly focus on the instruments; it seemed as though the engine was trying to tear itself loose from its bearers. I must land, and quickly. I looked down at the undulating countryside, enmeshed in a tightly woven net of stone walls and winding lanes; there was no chance of landing without damaging the machine, and I was determined not to do that.

I throttled back even more as the vibration intensified; perhaps if I was really careful I could keep her in the air as far as Swansea, but that meant either a slight detour or the last 5 miles across the bay to the Gower peninsula – that decision could wait for a while.

Every now and then a heavy jarring shock similar to the first made me flinch; I had no idea of what was going on in the engine compartment, except that I was steadily losing power, and now the oil pressure was falling. I became worried about the possibility of fire, and I realised that while I might risk my own neck I could not jeopardise the safety of my passenger sitting isolated in the front seat, and with whom I could not communicate – the machine was not equipped with intercom.

I searched for some kind of landing ground, but it was impossible. With the speed down to 55 knots, and barely maintaining height, I edged slowly towards the coast, for it was here, many years ago, that racing-car pioneers had captured world records for speed along the Pendine Sands, a long stretch of beach made of hard-packed sand, deserted now save for the ghost of Parry Thomas, who had been decapitated at the wheel of his giant racing car 'Babs' when a driving chain broke.

One could easily land a jet aircraft on this beach – if only the engine would hold long enough for me to reach it. As the oil pressure fell, the vibration intensified. I was horrified to see the wingtips flapping up and down about 6 inches – and this on an externally braced biplane! I could no longer maintain height, for the engine no longer responded to increased throttle demands. Down, down, and the coast seemed no nearer; gone now were thoughts of landing on the beach.

The other aircraft, aware that something was badly amiss, had sheared off. Well, a field it would have to be, I thought, when out of the corner of my eye I saw a windsock! There were no airfields here; it must be a private strip. Anyway, it didn't matter – any port in a storm. I throttled back, and as if to confirm my decision the engine gave a mighty bang and stopped. I switched off fuel and ignition; with only 800 feet left to go there was no time to assess the situation. The windsock gave me the direction of approach, and as I looked at the field properly for the first time I became aware that it seemed incredibly small for a farmer's private airstrip; in fact, it wasn't a strip as much as a square plot of levelled ground with buildings and trees on two sides, while a road and houses bounded the third.

I realised that I would have to make a really accurate approach if I was to have any hope of stopping, so I started a gentle sideslipping turn with the slipstream moaning eerily through the wires, the propeller stiff and straight like a sentry on guard duty.

The only good thing about it was that the engine had not caught fire. In the turn the windscreen was opaque, and I realised that the whole aeroplane was covered with oil – I later discovered that No 2 cylinder head had split in two!

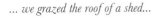

... we grazed the roof of a shed...

The landing run looked impossibly short, I sideslipped hard, speed 40 knots, the aircraft shuddered on the verge of a stall, but I held her hard in the sideslip. The tailwheel flicked through the topmost branches of a tree, we grazed the roof of a shed, as I kicked her straight an instant before she touched. Fish-tailing hard, braking left and right with the tail kicking, she stopped mere feet from the far hedge. People rushed across the field.

'Small airfield you've got here,' I said.

'Oh,' was the reply, 'its not an airfield, its a helicopter pad!'

9

I sit in the cockpit, in silence, trying to stop my legs from shaking – that could have been the end of sixteen years' work.

Parking Ticket for a Pup

WITH wires wailing eerily, the little biplane knifed through the summer air, the sun sparkling and glinting on the immaculate finish of our Pitts S1.S Special. Light and sensitive to the touch, this flight was unusual in two respects: first, the aircraft was flying straight and level, instead of snarling through an aerobatic sequence, and second, the purpose of the flight was to become acquainted with another biplane, totally different in concept and performance. I was about to turn the clock back to the dark days of the First World War, and to have the chance of comparing my modern, tremendously strong biplane with a frail predecessor, for I had been asked to flight-test a 1916 Sopwith Pup, which had been carefully restored over a period of 16 years.

Braced against the high acceleration, I held the little Pitts in a wide arc over the field, and there, on the grass, incongruous amongst the modern tricycle trainers, stood the Pup, its RFC roundels stark against the olive-green fabric.

Over the hedge at 100mph with the scream of the wires dying to a murmur as she touched down, hard on the brakes to slow her wild progress. I taxied alongside the Pup, admiring the skill and care that had gone into this restoration. From being a small fragile craft it seemed quite large by comparison with my gaudily painted transport, though its span is only a little over 26 feet. Rocking slightly in the gentle breeze as though impatient to be once again in the air, the Pup was the centre of attraction, as the modern types seemed to fade into the background.

But to business. Today was the proving engine run and, if successful, it would give the all-clear for the first flight. Although some of the material was new, the basic aircraft was already well experienced long before I was born, with quite a few enemy aircraft to its credit.

The preparations for starting a rotary engine are akin to some primitive rite. First, large chocks must be found; small ones won't do because the aircraft will climb straight over them. Then all the plugs must be cleaned with meths – petrol won't do because it just mixes with the castor oil. When they are all installed and the HT wires connected, the petrol must be turned on until the system floods, and finally each cylinder (nine in all) must be primed with a large and very unpleasant-looking syringe. Following this procedure the mixture must be given the benefit of several rotations of the engine, and the attempted start must be carried out immediately. The petrol cock is left off until the engine actually fires, otherwise everything becomes drowned with fuel and one has to dry out the plugs and start all over again.

I was to be a spectator on this occasion while Des, the owner, sat in the cockpit. Mike, the engineer on the project, grasped the propeller firmly and called 'Contact'. Putting all his strength into it, he gave a mighty swing, and with a roar and a cloud of blue smoke, the Le Rhone started. The next few moments are always critical as one juggles with the engine controls. There are two levers, one controlling the air supply, the other, called the 'fine adjustment', controlling the petrol flow by means of a needle valve.

One has to change the relationship of these levers for every power setting, and also for changes of attitude, altitude, speed and temperature. Also, the engine will not run at all below about 800rpm, with a maximum ground rpm of about 1,100. So for low-power settings one has to control the rpm with an ignition cut-out button on the stick. While Des was getting the engine to run steadily, I made the first mistake of the day by standing alongside the fuselage to look into the cockpit, because a rotary engine in action dispenses dirty castor oil without fear or favour, and I have yet to find a dry-cleaner who can remove the results effectively.

Since one cannot run a rotary engine on the ground for very long without melting it, there was barely time to note the lever positions for various settings before it had to be shut down. One cannot just let things cool down, then start up again – one has to follow the complete procedure and, since things were running late, we had to postpone the first flight, but at least all systems were go!

As the Pitts climbed away like a homesick angel I wondered what my next biplane take-off would be like from that airfield – in a machine that hadn't flown for fifty-seven years! I was soon to find out, and the contrast turned out to be shattering, to say the least.

Mike turned the prop slowly, squirting neat petrol into the cylinders. The engine gurgled and wheezed as only a rotary can, but this time I could not see what he was doing. My view was practically obliterated by the vast round cowling, the flat, well-padded windscreen and the fat Vickers with its cocking lever still in position. The cockpit was cramped and uncomfortable. I couldn't see more than half the instruments without contorting myself round that infernal gun mechanism. The engine controls were well forward and I had to twist in my straps to reach them properly. And they actually went to war in machines like this?

'Ready?' said a voice from the bows. I adjusted the levers hopefully.

'Contact,' said the voice. I put the switch up. The propeller spun, propelled by an unseen hand. As it slowed I was about to switch off when there was a cough followed by a furious hissing roar. Blue smoke was everywhere and there was an overpowering stench of burnt castor oil. I remembered to turn on the fuel.

The engine immediately cut out, but the tremendous flywheel effect kept things spinning. I juggled anxiously with the levers, which resulted in a few spasmodic grunts from the front end, then, just as I thought it was going to stop, it leapt into life again. I experimented, and noted the lever positions that gave the highest rpm and the sweetest, cleanest note. I would need these for take-off. Throttling down as far as I dared, I 'blipped' the engine slowly and waved the chocks away. No taxiing here – we dare not risk oiling up the plugs – so we have already positioned the aeroplane for take-off. Now I can appreciate why they just took off straight from the hangars in the Great War.

Don't waste time – low rpm is critical. I release the cut-out and open up the air and petrol. As the Pup starts forward it is difficult to steer – the effects of the rotating engine are obvious, and the tailskid cannot be steered. The tail won't come up – the stick is fully forward, the engine sounds rough – something must be wrong. There's plenty of field ahead, wait a little longer, she's trying to swing, but now the tail is lifting and I can see ahead for the first time. She rolls easily over the grass, but there is no sign of life yet on the ASI. Acceleration is almost non-existent, but now we are getting airspeed and she feels lighter. Will she – won't she? Bounce, bounce, bounce – how slow she feels.

She's off! Still in the ground cushion, revs are too low. I fiddle with the levers. Come on, Pup! That's a little better, as I lean off the fine adjustment. 20 feet, 30 feet, struggling upwards – this can't be right.

I start a shallow turn to stay over the airfield – this lot could stop any second! My arm is aching – the nose is trying to rear up – she is terribly tail heavy. This is hard work – the controls are so stiff. Round and round, always over the field – and slowly, very slowly, upwards. I'm not getting enough power – I listen carefully to the engine. It doesn't sound as though it has a pot out. Is it too rich – or too lean? Round and round, fiddling with the engine controls, and all the time resisting its inclination to pitch up and stall. Thank heaven there is no turbulence today.

After 15 minutes I have had enough. At 1,000 feet I bring the Pup slowly to the stall. I must know this speed before landing, and I can get no higher; yet Pups used to fly to more than 20,000 feet! Petrol off, and with the engine dead, she handles a little better. There is no stall warning and at 37mph she nods gently – very ladylike. I open up the petrol – nothing happens. As I prepare for a forced landing the engine picks up. I later discover that it takes 7 whole seconds from opening up the fine adjustment before anything happens up front!

With 800rpm the Pup settles down at 50mph downwind. The forward pressure on the stick is easier, but I still have to use two hands every few minutes. I leave the levers set and use the ignition cut-out, but not for too long at any one time in case of fuel pooling with the subsequent fire hazard. I have enough trouble without that!

The Pup curves steeply towards the field. Blip, blip. Careful now, exactly into wind, remember the narrow track, remember the short-travel bungee undercarriage, remember the fixed tailskid, remember the high nose-up attitude on the ground, remember... Good Lord, it's down! Just as I'm thinking what an easy aeroplane it is to land, it swings! Full rudder, but I can't stop it, and it curves gently through 90 degrees before it stops. Well, at least I kept the engine going, I think, as Mike races across the field to help me taxi.

Over the next few weeks we tried everything. New plugs, modifications to fuel system linkage, new prop – that was nearly a disaster, since it was a coarser pitch and she just would not fly. I cut the switch and put it back on the ground.

There had to be a solution; after all, it was only a very simple aeroplane. One thing was sure, we were not getting enough power, although everything appeared to be perfect. Several times we pushed the aircraft all the way across the airfield, spent 3 hours trying to start it, without success, and pushed it all the way back again. Only one minor fault was ever noted; sometimes some of the plugs were oiled up. One day we realised that they were always in the odd-numbered cylinders, and this clue led us to the slip-ring, which was found to be wrongly installed.

By now I had had half a dozen rather hairy flights, during some of which the aeroplane had been dumped rather unceremoniously back on the aerodrome. So it was that I approached the machine warily following rectification of this last snag. The engine sounded strong enough on the chocks, but I wasn't going to be fooled again!

The chocks were pulled away and I opened up. I don't know who was the more surprised, myself or the small band of enthusiasts on the ground. The tail came up immediately, and I just had time to catch the swing before she was in the air. I leaned off a fraction to prevent the normal rich cut (killed a lot of Camel pilots, that did), and up she went. With the new power she was impossibly tail-heavy and with the stick hard forward it was 1,500 feet before she levelled off.

And did she go! Now I could really feel the gyroscopic effects of the rotary engine at full power. After 15 minutes I thought I ought to land, as this was the first time we had used that much power.

Mike examined the engine, which was apparently exceedingly healthy. Drunk with success, we embarked on another flight. We should have known better! Just after take-off, it quit, stone dead!

Should I land straight ahead, or risk turning back? An agonising decision, but the ground was impossible ahead – the Pup would not survive. To hesitate would be to lose my only chance; I started to turn. The wind was very strong that day, and as I turned I had to lower the nose further and further to maintain airspeed. A blister hangar swung into view, but for the moment I must ignore it – I must only think of flying accurately, not giving away an inch of precious height. The hangar looms large in the windscreen, but I keep turning, steadily, gently. The ground speed increases with the wind behind, I lift a wing to clear the hangar, the field is ahead – but downwind! Now is the time to be bold and firm. With the left wing down to contain the drift, I drive the Pup on to the ground with the tail up. I use the controls hard and initially she runs straight before the tailwind catches her. But I have held her long enough, and her speed has almost gone. She swings through 90 degrees, and stops. I sit in the cockpit, in silence, trying to stop my legs from shaking – that could have been the end of sixteen years' work.

We can find nothing wrong with the engine, but we increase the size of the fuel lines and readjust the primitive carburettor. The weeks go by and finally we are again ready for an air test. Inexplicably she performs even better than she has ever done before, and the carburettor adjustment allows much more control over the engine.

On this sortie we have planned to take some air-to-air photographs from a Stampe. Dave, the Stampe pilot, is astonished to find that he cannot keep up in the climb! At 50mph the Pup is climbing at 1,200 feet per minute!

The last test flight is over – the Pup is ready to move to its new home at

Blackbushe, but first it has to go to Redhill. Confident now of her performance, I set off. The engine is sweet and strong and she cruises at nearly 100mph. Ahead the clouds look dark and forbidding, but with only 10 miles to go I press on. With no compass, I am concentrating on map-reading when I notice that it is starting to rain. Soon I am unable to see through the windscreen and I have to lean right out of the cockpit, into the stinging rain, now turning to sleet. Castor oil blurs my goggles, and the sleet burns like fire on my face. It is hard to breathe against the icy blast, and I am grateful to be able to throttle down for the landing. I find that my forehead is bleeding, cut by tiny ice particles, but I am more concerned for the propeller, which is slightly eroded for the same reason. Fine glasspaper and a coat of varnish soon puts things right, and finally, reluctantly, I must fly the Pup to Blackbushe, to its final home in the new museum.

No longer is it a lethal, primitive machine, for now I have come to accept it as a reliable aeroplane.

On the way I am again accompanied by Dave in the Stampe, this time with a photographer armed with a colour cine-camera, to record the occasion. There is a little haze, so I climb higher and higher to reach better photographic conditions. The Pup rides steadily on the cold, crisp winter air, and the photographer starts filming. Now he smiles, and waves – he has some good coverage, and he can go home.

I close the fine adjustment, and start downwards towards less Arctic conditions. After 1,000 feet I open up to clear the engine, but nothing happens! I set course for the nearest aerodrome, but unless the engine gives some power I will never make it. I try all the tricks I know to coax a rotary engine into life, but it is absolutely dead. For over a minute I glide with the petrol off and the air wide open – now I know it cannot be over-rich, but still it will not run. At 50mph the Le Rhone spins freely at 350rpm, in deathly silence apart from the humming of the wires.

The Stampe is alongside, its crew obviously worried. I wave it away. I have checked everything – it isn't going to restart. At 1,000 feet I turn off the petrol and switch off the magneto. I have selected my field, in the grounds of a large house. There is a cricket pitch marked out, therefore it must be smooth and level; I must not damage the aeroplane. There is no wind so I select the best approach. The wires moan and whine as I sideslip off the last bit of height. I let her straighten, and she floats over a 6-foot hedge, between two trees, and sits delicately down on the grass. Look out – the cricket pitch is roped off, there are metal stakes!

I rudder hard, crazily the Pup slithers through the gap, swings through the inevitable 90 degrees, and stops. She is safe. The owner of the house is friendly and hospitable. It is too late to do anything today so we picket the machine in the shelter of some buildings.

A policeman arrives. 'Is this a forced landing?' he asks.

'Yes,' I reply.

Later I amuse myself by thinking of all the other possible answers! He wants to see my pilot's licence, which I don't have with me. He then proceeds to write out a ticket, requiring me to produce my licence at a police station! I think he is joking and start to laugh. He is not joking and is obviously not amused. I decide to let him get on with it and to carry out the proper procedure myself, later. He says he knows all about forced landings because he has flown in a glider. I am careful not to laugh. He departs. The owner of the land invites us back to the house for a drink. Some of the groundcrew look as though they need it.

Next morning we check the aircraft. She has more than half a tank of fuel, the plugs are clean; there is apparently nothing wrong. I believe that the air pressure in the tank could not equalise during the descent and therefore caused a suction on the fuel, preventing it from flowing. The fuel tank cap air vent is certainly small. I pace the field – more than 300 yards. Plenty for a Pup. We decide to try the engine – after all, either one has full revs and can take off, or one doesn't. She starts second swing and roars at full power, sweet and clean. Chocks away, and I give her full power. In seconds she has gone, leaving behind a haze of castor oil and swirling oak leaves.

The engine hums sweetly and the Pup cruises with her tail well up. Blackbushe is expecting us, and as I circle over the field a green light shines from the tower. Today the Pup behaves herself and taxies in demurely. The press are there to meet us. The Le Rhone sighs to a halt. Photographs are taken. A reporter comes up, stares at the castor oil dripping from the engine.

'Did you have any trouble with such an old aeroplane?' he asks.

I look at the poised pencil and notepad. 'No, not really,' I answer.

I have come to like this Pup.

10

Very much aware of the lurid tales surrounding the aeroplane, I lined up into what little wind there was and opened the throttle wide.

Voyage of the Humming Bird

'THIS little machine has shown itself to possess an excellent all-round performance, to be extremely easily handled, both on the ground and in the air, and to be capable of all forms of 'stunting'. It has been flown in the worst of weather and has demonstrated that either as a sporting single seater or as a training machine, it can take the place of much more expensive and powerful types.'

So runs a contemporary account of the de Havilland 53 Humming Bird light monoplane in the *Flying Encyclopaedia* for 1923.

By the autumn of 1973 DH 53 G-EBHX had achieved the somewhat uninspiring record of 5 hours 30 minutes total flying and three major crashes since it was built 50 years earlier. Its last unpremeditated descent had been a particularly severe one. The engine had seized up after take-off; burning stubble fields ahead made the ensuing crash inevitable. The various components were collected and transported to White Waltham for restoration, while the offending engine was despatched to Rolls-Royce at Leavesden where its behaviour was investigated by Dr Moult and his team of experts.

There was evidence enough from the twin pistons of the 42hp ABC Scorpion, for they were heavily scored, as were the cylinder liners. Clearly the alloy pistons, already hot from ground running, could not stand the extra temperature and reduced cooling of the take-off and climb. A fix had to be found. The pistons were cleaned up and the cylinders honed out until there was a clearance of approximately 0.020 inch, the same as a Gipsy Major. Then the engine was thoroughly inspected, assembled and run.

Back at White Waltham, Jim Kelly and Pete Baston completed a mammoth rebuild of the airframe, which had taken five years of spare-time work. On 7 November 1973 the first flight was made by Air Commodore Allen Wheeler, Custodian of the Shuttleworth Collection to which the

Humming Bird now belongs. He remarked that the characteristics coincided very accurately with his recollections of a similar machine some 40 years previously. Then I was invited to fly it and, if tests proved satisfactory, to arrange for it to be ferried back to Old Warden Aerodrome in Bedfordshire where the Shuttleworth Collection is based.

Although the DH 53 was only a 'simple little aeroplane', the fact that it had averaged 1 hour every ten years, and had still contrived to come to grief in spectacular fashion three times, made me approach the project with some caution.

The cockpit, though cramped, was fairly comfortable. There was no real nose reference, the nose itself being practically non-existent. Instruments were minimal, with a solitary gleaming brass switch dominating the panel to control the single magneto. Fuel and oil tanks were immediately aft of the tiny engine, fuel capacity being a ridiculous 2 gallons.

The starting sequence, begun before the pilot boarded the aircraft, resembled some primitive rite. First the fuel was selected on, following which the tail was lifted at arm's length for half a minute or so, then it was shaken bodily for a few seconds before being lowered to the ground. This was the moment for the pilot to climb in. At the same time the exhaust pipes, each of which stood up like the twin smoke stacks of a Mississippi paddle steamer, were carefully dosed with one teaspoonful of neat gasoline. The brass magneto switch was turned on and the propeller spun vigorously. This was accompanied by barks and wheezes, and on one terrifying occasion two yellow tongues of flame licked hungrily towards the cockpit. At last the engine shuddered into life, spitting and belching black smoke. Its behaviour grew less alarming at full power, with a loud exhaust crackle, as though it were trying to make up in noise for what it lacked in thrust.

Finally the great moment arrived. Very much aware of the lurid tales surrounding the aeroplane, I lined up into what little wind there was and opened the throttle wide.

Anticlimax reigned supreme – it refused to move! With the engine still at full power, the stick was eased forward to take the weight off the skid and the rudder waggled vigorously. This unusual combination, learned many years ago from another ultra-light type, was the key to the problem, and the little aeroplane reluctantly started forward.

Owing to the lack of nose reference it was difficult to find the correct attitude for the take-off run; I had to achieve a delicate balance between aerodynamic drag with the tail too low, and undercarriage drag with the tail too high. An occasional backward glance gave a fairly good indication of pitch attitude at this stage. The tiny, narrow wheels sank into the soft grass and eventually the machine stabilised at about 35mph. This would never do, especially as we were by now halfway across the aerodrome... However, there was still plenty of time, and sure enough, when the aircraft encountered a small bump, it was neatly propelled into the air. Thereafter the speed built up reasonably well. On subsequent take-offs I found that by lifting the tail very much higher during the early stages the ground run, although still prolonged, was improved.

In the smooth air, just after take-off, I noticed that the ailerons were tramping very slightly. I determined to investigate this further. The phenomenon disappeared as speed was increased and the aircraft settled into the climb, the Scorpion flogging away for all it was worth. Still alert for any

tricks it might play, I manoeuvred so that I could land on the airfield at any
time should the engine stop. This performance must have driven ATC nearly
to distraction as I wandered irregularly about. Finally I achieved a safe height
and continued to climb in slow wide spirals. The engine, very underpowered
it seemed, vibrated continuously but showed no particular signs of distress.

   The aircraft responded briskly to control movements, the ailerons being
particularly powerful. Maximum speed in level flight at 2,400rpm was
65mph, and the aeroplane was slightly nose-heavy, no trimmer being
available. As speed was reduced towards the stall it was noticeable that when
ailerons were used there was a tendency for them to trail in the direction of
roll, and for such a little aeroplane there was considerable inertia in the
aileron circuit. This obviously needed further investigation. A slow stall
approach gave lateral rocking at 45mph, followed by a 'g' break at 42mph.

During the rocking the ailerons were trying to snatch towards the dropping wing. When the ailerons were held firmly the nose dropped gently and cleanly at the stall, but when held lightly they snatched to the right coincident with a sharp wing drop through 90 degrees. This behaviour was also apparent as the dynamic stall was approached, and during fast roll reversals. It was only at very high angles of attack just prior to the stall that it was noticeable, and could be corrected by a firm grip on the stick.

Part of the reason for the DH 53's bad reputation was now beginning to come to light. Sideslips were made to assess stability and, although the aircraft behaved normally at low sideslip values, as these were increased first the ailerons, then the rudder, suffered a force reversal, and the ailerons had to be deflected in the opposite sense to maintain the sideslip, demonstrating marked lateral instability in this mode. This was perhaps the second link in the chain. I next carried out some general handling and found that, despite this interesting behaviour, provided the machine was flown with a firm hand it responded in a brisk and lively manner. These peculiarities, having once been sampled at a safe height, fell into their proper perspective; but at low level, just after take-off, with the additional complication of an engine failure, would be no place to discover them for the first time.

I was just beginning to sit back and enjoy myself when the oil pressure decided to fall. The engine showed no signs of ailing; I was even getting used to the vibration! It was obvious that the pressure was going to vanish before I could land so I removed the need for further decisions by switching off, whereupon the propeller stopped.

'Now I'm for it,' I thought, with lurid tales of brick-like gliding angles springing to mind. Again, anticlimax! At 55mph the little aeroplane glided at about the same angle as a throttled-back Tiger Moth. I even had to slip a little height off at the last moment, and there was plenty of control left to flare and settle on three points.

Adjustments were made to the oil pressure relief valve, and off we went again. This time the take-off run, with the tail a little higher initially, was more reasonable. ATC again suffered my wanderings around the circuit (for I was determined not to be caught out if the engine stopped) until eventually a safe height was reached. Again the oil pressure fell and the engine was switched off, and again the gliding angle was quite reasonable. During the ensuing sideslip it was noted that the control force reversal was not present with the propeller stopped.

Finally, after several adjustments, the oil pressure more or less behaved itself. During a normal approach to land it was slightly embarrassing to find that the aircraft had an extremely flat glide, which was not helped by the fact that the engine had to be set at a rather fast tick-over to keep it running at all. Once on the ground, however, the high drag of the undercarriage brought the machine to a halt in a very short distance indeed.

We had decided that following a trouble-free flight of 30 minutes it would be possible to plan the ferry flight back to Old Warden. So, on 21 January 1974 the Humming Bird set out on its journey home. There was high cloud cover, but the visibility was excellent. It was also very cold. One large orbit of the field was made at 800 feet to give the engine its final option of quitting, but it crackled away as though it really meant business, and 2,200rpm gave a cruising speed of 57mph.

Eventually there was nothing for it but to forsake the safety of White Waltham and to point the nose at Booker, some 11 miles to the north. There I would fuel and would be met by Jim Kelly and Air Commodore Wheeler, who, having seen me off, would make the journey by road to coincide with my arrival. There was no such refinement as a compass. However, on a clear winter's day I expected no problems so long as the engine kept running.

Slowly the countryside flowed beneath the wings, while I selected field after field against the possibility of a forced landing. But the engine had never sounded better, and soon I found myself gliding around the final turn, close in and with plenty of height in hand. At the pumps I asked for the tank to be topped up. The mechanic's face was a study when he found it would only take 5 pints! After lunch we returned to find the DH 53 surrounded by incredulous onlookers, whose ribaldry turned to thoughtfulness when they discovered the fuel consumption.

Now for the first time I was able to take off on a hard runway, and what a difference it made. Full control and reasonable acceleration from the start... I was able to unstick cleanly before I passed the Air Commodore, who was positioned 150 yards down the runway, armed with his camera to record the occasion.

Taking a bearing from the runway as I flew back overhead, I settled down for the longest leg of the day – 18 miles to Leavesden, via Bovingdon. Eventually the hangars of Bovingdon appeared over the bows. I reflected on the last time I had flown from here, in a Mosquito. How different that powerful beast from its tiny predecessor. But now the airfield was deserted, and of no use to me except as an emergency landing ground… Wait, though, it can still help me, for here I must turn for Leavesden. The runways are still painted, so using this rudimentary compass, and estimating the angle of my track, I roll out on the new heading.

Now the Humming Bird is affected by a slight headwind, which cuts down its already very low ground speed. I remember a tale of a DH 53 years ago in Belgium where to the pilot's disgust it was overtaken by a train. The engine chugs away steadily. Why was it called a Humming Bird, I wonder. We are so slow that we seem to hover; a speck in the distance materialises into a modern light plane, which flashes past a few hundred yards away; even its mediocre speed seemed alarming by contrast with our snail-like progress. He doesn't see me.

Cold sets in, and I begin to shiver. At last Leavesden appears ahead. I decide to land on the grass, uphill towards the north-east, and as I spiral lower a green light shines from the tower. A careful sideslip to get rid of height, and as I straighten I switch off the engine. Now the glide is normal, and in the flare I 'blip' the engine just as if I were controlling a rotary. This gives no more than a short float and an early touchdown.

The programme now called for a stay at Leavesden of about a week, so that the Rolls-Royce apprentices could see what sort of an aeroplane was propelled by the engine they had helped overhaul. To say that they were thunderstruck would be an understatement. From here the machine was to be flown at Hatfield, home of de Havilland before the merger with Hawker Siddeley Aviation, and it was fitting that an HSA test pilot should fly it for this leg.

On the appointed day, after some initial difficulty in starting, the ground run was satisfactory, so a telephone call was made to Hatfield. This produced Des Penrose, complete with flat hat (to be worn backwards) and Mk 8 goggles. Thus attired he was soon installed in the DH 53 and pointed in the direction of the runway. Well content with our efforts, I returned home.

Later that day the telephone rang. It was Des. Apparently as he was passing Radlett Aerodrome the Scorpion came out in sympathy with the now sadly defunct Handley-Page company, and quietly died. With more than 7,000 feet of runway under him, it seemed the obvious place to go, so down he went. 'Couldn't happen to a nicer chap,' I said, totally lacking in concern. A ground run seemed OK so he launched off once again, but although Hatfield was only 4 miles away the Scorpion was determined to remain at Radlett, where eventually the Humming Bird was wheeled into a hangar, now practically empty save for the ghosts of Hastings, Herald, Victor and Jetstream.

An inspection failed to reveal anything significant. With some misgivings, therefore, the machine was wheeled out a day or so later and had its minute tank topped up. Inexplicably the engine behaved normally, and after orbiting Radlett for some time Des Penrose set out across country. It was with some relief that he finally dropped the Humming Bird on to the grass beside the control tower at Hatfield.

Now all that remained was to embark on the final leg of the journey to Old Warden, 20 miles away to the north. It was clear that so long a flight couldn't be attempted without a more thorough look at the engine, so over the next few months the experts delved into the mystery of the reluctant Scorpion. During this period Des Penrose left the company to become a commercial pilot. I personally think that he fled rather than embark on another epic in the DH 53!

Evidently the pistons had again been scored; it was apparent that the clearances were still not sufficient. The cylinders were honed out, and a Ki-gass priming pump was fitted, as it was thought that by priming through the exhaust system the oil had been washed off the liners. Most important, the little engine appeared to need all of its 2-gallon head of fuel to ensure safe operation during the take-off and climb.

Obviously it would be a pity to disturb it.

So it was that on a July morning I received a telephone call from Ron Clear, who had been in charge of these modifications, to inform me that the aeroplane was ready for collection. I turned up at the flight sheds to find the DH 53 nestling between a Mosquito and a Cirrus Moth. Obviously it would be a pity to disturb it. I peered into the cockpit; yes, there was the Ki-gass pump modification. I scowled suspiciously at the engine – it looked just the same as it always did.

With a rumble the hangar doors opened and willing hands pushed the machine out. A crowd of onlookers materialised from nowhere, looking expectant. I climbed aboard and gave the engine a shot via the Ki-gass. 'Contact,' said the mechanic, and spun the propeller. Nothing happened. Just as I was beginning to think I was reprieved, the engine gave a mighty snort and burst into life. At first it wouldn't run below 1,800rpm, which gave so much vibration that I could hardly focus on the instruments. It had a monumental flat spot between slow running and half throttle, and from the twin exhaust stacks there issued a veritable cacophony of bangs, splutters and coughs.

It's difficult to do a magneto check when there is only one, so I thought I had better get going before something melted. With assistants on the wingtips I was finally aligned into the wind. I opened the throttle and was horrified by the cloud of black smoke that was hurled skywards; however, this soon cleared, and the tiny machine started to move. I didn't really care what sort of noises came from the front end just so long as they kept coming.

It was a day of large cumulus clouds and good visibility. The last leg of the journey had begun! Slowly we climbed to 2,000 feet, where I let the speed increase to 57mph at 2,200rpm. The engine, by comparison with a modern power unit, rattled and vibrated in a shocking manner, but I had now come to accept this vibro-massage as normal Scorpion operation. Perched at the front of the machine, I had time to see every detail on the ground and to note the overtaking speed of the traffic on the A1 Motorway below – all the more evident because of the north wind.

Slowly we crawl across the vast dome of the sky, giving Luton and its airport a very wide berth. In the distance a jet flashes across and I am alarmed in case it comes my way – I cannot get out of its path if it does. But it turns away. I note that the oil pressure is falling slowly and wish I had an oil temperature gauge. Navigation is no problem; I know this part of the country well, though I had not realised how many golf courses there are near Stevenage.

Now Baldock is in sight as I swing back towards the north-west. My ground distance will be more like 25 miles, but I make sure that I can always reach a safe landing area. I relax a little as I reach Henlow, an RAF base – only 5 more miles to go, with the oil pressure still within limits though dropping slowly. Here I can land without difficulty should the engine stop, but no, it seems determined to keep going. We rattle on northwards for several minutes when I glance down and notice a jet aeroplane on the ground. I am at a loss to know what an aircraft could be doing there; then it dawns on me, I am still over Henlow!

And at last, Old Warden – always hard to detect from the air among the woodlands of Bedfordshire. There is a familiar copse of trees on the south side of the aerodrome. As I get within gliding distance I inform the engine that it may now quit if it wants to. It refuses to do so, and clatters away merrily. The oil pressure has stabilised at 18psi. I turn over the hangars, the DH 53 pivoting exuberantly on a wingtip, for she has completed a flight of more than 60 miles in less than six months.

The Voyage of the Humming Bird is over.

11

The moaning and whistling of the engines had been replaced by a muffled roar like a distant waterfall. I pulled back hard on the stick, and at 100 knots she slowly and ponderously rotated and smoothly lifted off the runway.

Meteor

FROM the ceiling of the Science Museum in London hangs an ugly little aeroplane with a large letter 'P' for Prototype painted on the fuselage. Though insignificant in appearance, it represented in its day a remarkable step forward in aviation technology, for it was the first British jet. This little stubby aeroplane, the Pioneer, paved the way for its successor, the twin-jet Meteor, Britain's first front-line jet fighter, and the mainstay of the RAF's fighter squadrons in the early 1950s.

Both the Pioneer and early Meteors were powered by Whittle jet engines of low thrust, and although the Pioneer could achieve more than 300 knots at 20,000 feet, until engine thrust could be increased from 860lb to more than 2,000lb there was no chance of a successful single-engined fighter. Hence the twin-engined Meteor. Gloster had some real headaches in those days, because no one had any experience of jet operation. The Meteor was so very different in appearance from the Pioneer because of the problem of where to install the engines; should they be enclosed in the fuselage, underslung, or in nacelles? Nacelles were chosen for best accessibility for maintenance, but they also meant that the tailpipe had to be fed through the rear spar of the wing. The Pioneer, because of the lack of propeller weight and the rear location of its engine, had employed a tricycle undercarriage, and this was designed into the Meteor for the same reason. It seems strange to us now that any jet aircraft should have been fitted with a tailwheel undercarriage (as was the Attacker), but it seems that this was a real possibility in the early days at Gloster.

During the initial design of the Meteor in 1940 the Pioneer had still not yet flown, so very little was known about the effect of the exhaust gases around the tail unit. It was therefore decided to mount the tailplane well up on the fin, in spite of misgivings about the structural strength of this configuration.

Engine thrust was still a matter for concern, as acceleration was far too slow for test flying to begin, so an order was placed for engines of increased power. Shortly after this the Ministry of Aircraft Production ordered Gloster to stop work on the production aircraft because of the failure of the engine manufacturer to keep to its delivery dates, a common enough occurrence these days, but a staggering blow during the war. Fortunately another engine had been designed by Major Halford's team at de Havilland, and two of these engines were made available to get the prototype Meteor airborne. Various engines were fitted from time to time in Meteors, even the turbo-prop Trent engine (as a test installation), and the Armstrong Siddeley Sapphire, as well as Avons, Nenes and Metrovick Beryls, but the main power-plant was the Rolls-Royce Derwent.

The Meteor saw action at the end of the war, and continued to be developed during the post-war period as a fighter, photo-recce, trainer, night-fighter and ground-attack aircraft. It gained prestige for Britain in 1946 by capturing the world airspeed record at 616mph. These days this may not seem terribly fast, but to ground observers and to the pilots of the High Speed Flight the impression of speed was very high. One reason for this was that at 500mph and above the Meteor produced a sound we used to call the 'blue note'. This was a classic Doppler effect, which swelled up into a crescendo as the hurtling machine passed by.

At high Mach numbers the Meteor had a mind of its own, and on one of the record attempts became so wing-heavy at speed that the pilot had to wedge his forearm between the side of the cockpit and the stick to prevent the aircraft from rolling and diving into the sea. At high altitude she had her tricks too: as speed was increased the nose-up change of trim became greater, until at around Mach 0.82 either wing might drop, or the trim might change nose-down to the accompaniment of heavy buffet. There was also a strong tendency to snake from side to side – altogether an uncomfortable ride. In the early days of squadron service pilots used to accept quite happily the fact that aileron snatch, vibration and general lateral misbehaviour was all part of the Meteor's high-Mach shock-wave effects, until one very startled pilot cottoned on to what was happening – it was a classic case of aileron flutter, and every aircraft was the same! The cause of aileron failures became apparent; it was only the Meteor's handling peculiarities that had allowed such a thing to go undetected.

Inevitably during its service career the Meteor was required to carry more equipment and armament, with the result that engine power had to be increased. Now the disadvantages of the wing-mounted engines became more critical, for the turning moment in the event of an engine failure had become very high, resulting in a safety speed of 165 knots on take-off. A very skilful and strong pilot might be able to control an engine failure at lower speeds than this, but if the failure occurred below 130 knots it was best to throttle back everything and land straight ahead. Also, since the hydraulic pump was on the right engine, if that engine should fail after take-off the unfortunate pilot was committed to staggering around the circuit with his left leg locked hard against the enormous rudder forces; indeed, it often became necessary to spare a hand to hold one's knee at top dead centre. A Meteor pilot after a session of asymmetric flying could hardly prevent his legs from trembling, and not always from the effects of the enormous rudder forces.

Another very nasty characteristic, especially with flaps up, was a phenomenon known as 'phantom diver'. If one kept the slip ball centred all was well but, if not, on occasion the aeroplane could enter a steep uncontrollable diving sideslip, which needed a lot of height to sort out. Since one usually encountered this on the downwind leg it was very often fatal. This was often abetted by the extension of the undercarriage, in that the left and nose wheels would sometimes lock down before the right wheel unlocked, initiating a yaw to the left. During my training days on Meteors this was a little-understood phenomenon, and it was not until many years later, on a twin-turboprop aircraft or similar tail layout, that the 'phantom diver' identified itself during a test flight, where the entire airflow on one side of the fin and on the underside of the tailplane turned through 90 degrees, then detached. The effect was as if one had lost half a tailplane and suffered an engine failure simultaneously, and was caused initially by a breakdown of flow at the junction of the fin and tailplane during a sideslip. While serving at Farnborough in the RAF I was able to produce this effect at a safe height by sideslipping with airbrakes out (which aggravated things), and losing 8,000 feet in the recovery!

By using harsh corrections one could keep the height loss down to 500 feet, but only by using full opposite rudder and pulling the stick hard back, to make the 'good' side of the tailplane do twice the work. It would have taken some nerve to do that at circuit height, but it was the only way to recover in time, should one encounter the dreaded 'phantom diver'. With the flaps down the airflow over the tail was altered, so there was less chance of a mishap. However, even with the slip ball centred, you could still get into trouble on one engine if you allowed the speed to get too low on finals, as with power increasing and speed falling there came a time when there wasn't enough leg strength or rudder power left, and the result was an uncontrollable yaw and roll. There is a story of a young fighter pilot who lost it on the approach, banged on full power on one engine, and carried out a complete uncontrolled barrel roll before demolishing the approach lights and arriving right way up on the runway with a battered but still intact aeroplane. The Meteor was very strong.

I had flown Meteors off and on throughout my service career, and regarded it with affection and nostalgia, in spite of its peculiarities, so I was delighted to receive a call from Doug Arnold at Blackbushe with the news that he had acquired a Meteor TT20 from Farnborough, asking me to collect it for him. Blackbushe already housed some immaculate Second World War piston aeroplanes (including Harvards, Sea Furies and a beautiful Mk XVI Spitfire) in the rapidly expanding museum, so the arrival of the Meteor would mark a natural progression.

With the target-towing winch, ventral and wing tanks, and long nose, it was much heavier than the earlier Marks I had been used to. Eight years had passed since I had last flown a Meteor, and that was the Mk 7 trainer, so I spent several days revising Pilot's Notes and looking at photographs of the cockpit. Eight years is a long time.

Finally the day arrived, and with it low cloud, rain and a healthy crosswind both at Farnborough and Blackbushe. Consoling myself with the thought that I would probably have both airfields much to myself, I walked into the hangar at Farnborough and got my first glimpse of the beast; it was much longer than the lighter types of Meteor I had been used to, and with all the tanks and the winch it looked more a projectile than an aeroplane. I was suddenly very conscious of how long it had been since I had last flown a jet fighter. I lowered myself into the cockpit, aware of the indefinable smell peculiar only to jets of that era; somehow the modern ones don't have that atmosphere. Controls, knobs, switches, all almost forgotten, became instantly familiar again as I looked at them and touched them. I had a minor panic trying to find the starter buttons – they had been moved from their original positions – then there was nothing else but to go. I pre-flighted in the hangar and signed the Form 700 as she was towed out.

As I strapped in and clipped on the oxygen mask the familiar starting routine came back. A mechanic unlocked the canopy latch and lowered it (all 274lb) into position. I closed the latches, and as they thudded home I felt completely isolated from the outside world. Left engine first: booster pump on, then press the starter button. For long seconds nothing happened, then a subdued whirring announced engine rotation – one then has to wait, of all things, for the undercarriage lights to dim with the increased secondary load, and this is the time to open the HP cock half-way, and wait for ignition. If this cock is opened too far or too quickly the resonance that results will rattle every window on the station. As engine speed increases above 2,000rpm one can open the cock fully, and the engine will then idle at 3,500rpm.

The same performance with the other engine, then trolley-acc and chocks away, instruments and compass switches on; as the R/T came to life I obtained taxi clearance. No time or fuel for prolonged checks – I had only 300 gallons in the main tanks, enough for just 30 minutes at low level. I checked the airbrakes and flaps as I taxied, noting the fast flap movement, and being very careful with the lever – it is next to the undercarriage lever! The brakes, operated by a lever on the stick, wailed in discord as only Meteor brakes can, and she rode soft and smooth on her big oleos and fat tyres. She was very nose-down as she taxied, so I could see everything ahead in spite of the extended nose.

There was nothing else flying as I lined up, the runway lights reflecting from pools of water; better watch for aquaplaning with these soft tyres, I thought.

Nose-wheel straight – no steering except by brakes and rudder when I had full power – and as the tower cleared me to go I opened slowly to 13,000rpm; checking temperatures and pressures, I released the brakes and applied full power, 14,550rpm. The acceleration was not noticeable as it is in a Spitfire, but was smooth and steady. I realised that I was pedalling the rudder, so I centralised it; it made no difference, she still ran straight. I pressed back on the stick, with no result as the speed reached 100 knots. The moaning and whistling of the engines had been replaced by a muffled roar like a distant waterfall. I pulled back hard on the stick, and at 100 knots she slowly and ponderously rotated and smoothly lifted off the runway. My hand moved quickly: brakes on, off, undercarriage up, throttle back to 14,100, flaps one-quarter down, power back to 12,500 as I turned on to the downwind leg – and I suddenly realised that I was at home in this aeroplane, as if there had never been that eight-year gap. I grew more confident and, though I had yet to land a TT20 for the first time, I had a good idea of what to expect. I

selected gear down, and automatically pressed right rudder to keep straight as
the left wheel lowered first. I could almost hear my old instructor say, 'Never
less than 7,500rpm until you're committed,' but at this weight I had 9,500rpm
as full flap went down, still in trim, and we crossed the black sheds at 130
knots. I had planned this first touch-and-go landing at 125 knots, a little fast
but better safe than sorry. I flared and throttled back and she sank on like a
feather – what a satisfying feeling – but you couldn't go wrong with such a
resilient undercarriage. As she touched I selected airbrakes out and lowered
the nose. I used the wheel brakes momentarily to feel their effect, then selected
airbrakes in and flaps (careful of the gear lever) up. Power on slowly, watching

rpm and jpt and listening for any resonance, and the eerie moan of the Derwents rose to a shriek, then to a muted roar as full power was achieved. In spite of the crosswind she had shown no real tendency to swing.

I made a few more circuits, with half-forgotten skills and confidence returning every second because I knew how she should fly, and I approached a little slower each time until I had the correct touchdown attitude and speed (112 knots) at the threshold. This time I braked to a full stop – no problem as long as I remembered that there was no anti-skid system. I checked the fuel, 70 gallons each side; it was time to go to Blackbushe. Again that slow sure acceleration, the reluctance to unstick, and this time I let her accelerate to 250 knots. There was a lot of inertia in both pitch and roll, and she jolted vertically quite heavily in the turbulence, so I throttled back and extended the airbrakes. Even at this relatively low speed the airbrakes give good deceleration, and I remembered how fierce they were at higher airspeeds, where one is really thrown forward in the straps. As the speed fell to 200 knots I selected a quarter flap; there is no point in selecting them at higher speeds because, although there is no speed limit, they have a relief valve that causes them to retract above 210 knots. I was very careful to close the airbrakes before selecting gear down – no 'phantom diver' today!

The runway at Blackbushe is not over-long – 1,290 metres – but I judged it long enough today, in spite of pools of water and a 90-degree crosswind, as long as I got the speed right. The runway in use was 08 with a right-hand circuit, so that the wind was behind me as I turned finals. The speed didn't decay quickly enough, and I was reluctant to fly a flatter approach or to lower flap earlier – an engine failure could have been a severe embarrassment! With only UHF I couldn't talk to Blackbushe tower, so everything had to be relayed through Farnborough.

Fuel state 40 gallons each side – that meant one attempt, then return to Farnborough. I decided to use 26; the wind seemed to be veering. The Meteor is a good stable aircraft on the approach and it's easy to hold an exact speed. On finals the crosswind was most evident, exaggerated by that long nose pointing like a weathervane into the wind. Everything looked right as she sank towards the threshold, and as I flared I cut the power and selected airbrakes out. She touched lightly and the nose dropped. I held the stick hard back and braked intermittently, the wail of the brakes blending with the deepening moan of the engines as she slowed and stopped, with about 250 metres of runway still to go. I suddenly realised that I'd been working; it was quite warm in the cockpit in spite of the cold and rain outside. I was also down to minimum safe fuel and my total flight time had been only 30 minutes – an expensive way to fly.

The Meteor has a place in history, not just as an exhibit in a museum, but as an aeroplane with that curious blend of virtues and vices we call character. Several exist; they can be kept airworthy, and with care they could be kept flying for years. And it was not so very hard to find a qualified Meteor pilot in 1976!

12

And then, somehow, I knew that something was not quite right. There was nothing I could put my finger on – speed, height, position, all were good. There was nothing material wrong at all, except that something was telling me not to do it.

The Day
I Should Have Died

IT happens, sooner or later, to almost everybody. Sometimes it's bad planning, or poor execution, or an error of judgement, or mechanical failure, or simply bad luck. Mostly it's the combination of two or more of these parameters, but the result is usually less nebulous: a broken machine, and maybe an injured pilot, or worse. Most general aviation pilots spend a large part of their aviation time in flight planning, or under supervision, in an attempt to stop events from ganging up on them, and they regard, often with dismay, the apparently death-defying performances put on at airshows by display pilots, who, in their eyes are an airborne version of 'Hell's Angels'.

By average pilot standards, display pilots would seem to be more at risk than they themselves are, puttering around in their Cherokee on a Sunday afternoon. What they probably do not consider is that these display pilots have a wider margin of safety available to them in spite of the apparently hazardous nature of their activity; also they are at least giving the job its required measure of concentration.

In fact, this comment really applies to the more experienced airshow pilots, who have been around long enough to have either made their own mistakes, or to have learned from the mistakes of others. There is also that younger breed of pilot, who, brimming with overconfidence, is sure it can never happen to him – until, one day, it does. And if he is one of the lucky ones, he will eventually fly again, as an older, sadder and wiser pilot.

Some years ago I was one of those young, overconfident display pilots, and I thought I could do a pretty good routine with a Stampe, at that time the only Gipsy-engined machine in the country. I was in training for the Lockheed Trophy, which was the big international contest of those days. Life was pretty good, and I was in constant demand at air shows up and down the country. My display routine was always the same: the 5-minute freestyle sequence I was practising for the Lockheed Trophy. It seemed to me that the final manoeuvre should be both novel and spectacular, so I had practised this at altitude for many weeks before I introduced it into my sequence. It was an inverted flick-roll from normal flight, so that one had to thrust the stick fully forward and kick on full rudder while flying at 85 knots at 400 feet. Thinking about it these days is enough to give me the shudders! But with the confidence of youth it worked, and was certainly spectacular, and some six weeks before the Lockheed Trophy was due to be flown off I was asked to demonstrate the Stampe at Biggin Hill. The aircraft being a two-seater, the membership secretary, a silver-haired old gentleman of vast aeronautical experience, asked me for a lift over to see the show, so we were soon airborne and heading for Biggin, in good time for briefing.

Here we were shown a map of the display line and were warned against flying over the crowd. In fact, most of the pilots (it was a long time ago, before the CAA got interested in this kind of thing) did fly over the crowd, and at low level as well. In the light of what happened, I am everlastingly thankful that I did not.

My turn came, in the middle of the afternoon, and with the knowledge that I had given the commentator a detailed briefing of my routine, I started. Everything was going well as I entered the last line on the sequence card and prepared for my new and wonderful manoeuvre, which I knew was already being described to the huge crowd of 80,000.

And then, somehow, I knew that something was not quite right. There was nothing I could put my finger on – speed, height, position, all were good. There was nothing material wrong at all, except that something was telling me not to do it. If that sort of thing happened these days, I would either do a four-point roll or some such simple manoeuvre, or perhaps even just pull up and gain height, but I was young and vain, and I thought stupidly that I should continue with the display. All I know is that I lost confidence at the last moment and that I did the manoeuvre anyway. Maybe because I had lost confidence I didn't hit stick and rudder as hard as I ought to have done; certainly I don't know, and I don't suppose anybody else does. The flick-roll started normally enough, but within half a turn it was starting to diverge in a most unpleasant way. I knew I was in trouble, and, too late, I realised the stupidity of what I had done. I put on full recovery control and left the throttle wide open to try and drag myself clear. At this stage, still in the manoeuvre, nobody else knew anything was wrong as I desperately tried to unstall the aeroplane. Too late, the nose pitched up and the aircraft entered an inverted flat spin, at 300 feet!

Now it was evident to all that I was in trouble, but the controls were beginning to bite, and the spin suddenly stopped, though with the nose pointing straight down. The ground was terrifyingly close, but I forced myself to keep cool. I would use every inch of available space to pull out, rather than risking a high-speed stall, but to no avail – the aircraft stalled twice in the pull-out, still at full power, and I recovered it twice. The ground seemed to leap upwards at me, and for more than a year afterwards I tasted fear every time the nose went down in low-level aerobatics. The ground ahead of me seemed clear, but there was a row of high trees I could not clear. Now the nose was up, though I was still banked to the left, and pulling hard. The aircraft was still sinking, mushing into the ground. I could not prevent it;

... the nose slammed down and the propeller exploded into a thousand flying fragments.

perhaps if the gear holds I can bounce and maybe clear the trees. She hit the ground hard with the port wheel and wingtip. The stick was hard back but the nose slammed down and the propeller exploded into a thousand flying fragments. The entire engine and nose section vanished and the fuselage cartwheeled as the wings crumpled around me. I was awestruck by the savage ferocity of the forces that were released – there seemed no end to the terrible noise of breaking wood and tearing fabric – and the bang of the initial impact echoed in my ears for months. I seemed to be turning over and over. I tried to protect my head at the expense of my arms – they would probably mend. Now the rending and crashing seemed more distant, and when I opened my eyes I realised that several minutes must have passed.

Not a sound could be heard, and as I focussed on the shattered wreckage I realised that I could see no colour, only black and white! I stared bemused, uncomprehending, and gradually shades of colour started to appear, and at the same time I began to hear noises around me, voices shouting, running footsteps. I released my harness and staggered to my feet, only then realising that my seat was several feet from the wreckage. Apparently the fuselage had broken when it was inverted and I had been ejected upwards and thrown clear only to be towed like a toboggan by the elevator cables, still in my seat, behind the sliding wreckage. The engine was buried underneath the wreckage, and beneath the engine was the cushion that had been behind my back; yet I was still strapped tightly into my seat. I looked at the secondary harness; it, too, had held, but attached to each strap was a piece of broken longeron! The front seat was squashed flat – no passenger could have survived. They carried me into the ambulance; for some reason they would not tell me if I had come down on any spectators, which caused me great stress, believing I had. In fact, I had crashed on the only uninhabited part of the airfield, behind one of the hangars. As the commentator put it, 'He's taken it behind the hangar' – there followed a great eruption of dust – 'and he's left it there'! Which did not endear the commentator to me when I eventually heard about it.

It is a strange experience to have an accident like that; it is as if one has a contagious disease. I lost many 'friends' overnight; indeed, only two people visited me in hospital. Perhaps it was because I was conceited, but whatever the reason it probably did me some good. I discharged myself and went back to the club. The membership secretary complained bitterly about having to walk home from Biggin, then took me up in a Tiger Moth to 'get my nerve back'. In fact, it was a

very long time before I got my nerve back, and from that day onwards I swore never to take any liberties with an aeroplane again. Sometimes I go back and look at that bit of ground behind that hangar – and I think of the way I was given another chance.

13

*Down, down, now we were only 10 feet over the standing
corn, the engine still pulling with all of its tiny heart.
And slowly, very slowly, again we started to climb.*

1912 Blackburn

ON 8 August 1908, at the small local racecourse at Hunaudieres, 5
miles south of Le Mans, there assembled a large gathering for the
purpose of witnessing an 'event'. This, the most critical of technical
audiences, had come from near and far, disbelieving and full of scepticism, to
see for themselves the much-publicised demonstration of flying by the
American aviator, Wilbur Wright. Although there had been several notable
flights by Europeans, the big difference was that on this side of the Atlantic
flight control was regarded as passive and corrective, an extension of
inherent stability; whereas the Wrights had progressed to using it as a positive
means of manoeuvre, as we see today in our modern aircraft. This had
allowed the Wrights a mastery of the air undreamed of in the Europe of
1908, so it was a crowd of suspicious sceptics who waited impatiently for the
big moment to arrive.

The machine was made ready, the engine started, and in the 2 minutes
that followed European aviation was revolutionised. It is difficult for us today
to understand the shock, dismay and stunned amazement that greeted the
American's effortless mastery of control, as he curved gracefully through the
air. The astounded French cried, 'We are beaten – we just don't exist. We are
as children compared with the Wrights,' and they wrung their hands in a
fervour of Gallic emotion.

There was applause, excitement, everybody was talking at once, so it
was hardly surprising that no one noticed a stolid, silent Yorkshireman
standing in the crowd. In the midst of pandemonium he stood, savouring the
impact of what he had just seen, his active brain already engaged on a
project that would earn him a place in history as a pioneer of British
aviation. His name was Robert Blackburn.

In common with most of the early pioneers, he was a determined man,
and one who made decisions quickly. He immediately left his job with a firm
of civil engineering consultants and devoted his life to aeronautics. It is

intriguing that although the Wright machine was a twin-screw pusher biplane, the aircraft that Blackburn designed and built was a single-airscrew tractor monoplane, similar in many respects to the Demoiselle, but of much more solid construction. In fact, it was so solid that it earned the title of 'Blackburn Heavy Type Monoplane'. The engine and pilot occupied a three-wheeled chassis, while the rest of the aeroplane was then apparently placed on top. There was a fixed tailplane, behind which was a cruciform aerodynamic structure, very much like the feathers of a throwing dart, which enjoyed full freedom of movement by means of universal joints – an all-moving elevator and rudder assembly.

This machine was transported to the sands near Saltburn, where, to use Blackburn's own words, he indulged in 'sand-scratching' – the Heavy Type Monoplane was indeed well-named!

Finally he achieved success, when the machine managed to rise from the beach on 24 May 1910, but alas his triumph was short-lived, as one of the landing wheels caught in a hole in the sand during a sideslip from an attempted turn. So ended the first Blackburn aeroplane. Undeterred, he tried a different approach. The Demoiselle layout was abandoned in favour of the more successful Antoinette layout, and the new machine was structurally more delicate, earning the title of 'Blackburn Light Monoplane'. Obviously an important lesson had been learned. Although the Gnome rotary engine was 'the' popular engine of the day, the new monoplane was powered by a small radial engine of 40hp with a 2.1 reduction gear to the propeller. One of the innovations was the adoption of a triangular fuselage section, a feature that was to remain a characteristic of all Blackburn aeroplanes up to 1914.

To avoid straining the wings through the warping control, the wings were pivoted about the rear spar. All the flying surfaces were connected to the steering wheel, leaving the feet free to operate the accelerator pedal on the floor, like a car. This machine flew very well, and was the real progenitor of the successful range of Blackburn monoplanes that followed.

B. C. Hucks, of Hucks starter fame, took his 'Mercury' (as the monoplane had now been renamed) on a tour of the West Country, making two crossings of the Bristol Channel and demonstrating wireless telephony at Cardiff from a height of 700 feet.

So popular had the Blackburn monoplanes become that in 1912 a machine was commissioned by a Mr Cyril Foggin for his personal use, the intention being to give exhibitions of flying – perhaps the first custom-built display aircraft? The general layout of the 'Mercury' was retained in the new machine, but many improvements were made, including the adoption of a pedal-operated rudder, such as we know today. Sheet aluminium was used for the front fuselage, and the empennage was modified to provide a one-piece rudder and divided elevators, a reversal of the previous technique. The cowling over the 50hp Gnome rotary was extended to afford the pilot better protection from the proliferation of oil and exhaust gases that all rotary engines dispense in the direction of the unhappy aviator.

The machine was delivered early in 1913, and Mr Foggin gave exhibition flights at Leeds. Shortly after this it passed into the hands of Mr Montague F. Glew, who flew it to his father's farm at Wittering, Lincs, where he crashed it. There it remained, broken and desolate, for some 25 years, when by a happy chance it was acquired by the Shuttleworth Collection and rebuilt to its original state.

At the end of the Second World War the Collection again began to organise open days, and on certain of these, when conditions were right, the Monoplane once again took to the air, but as the years passed it, in company with the Blériot and Deperdussin, was relegated to low straight hops across the airfield.

With its flying career drawing to a close, interest waned, particularly with the advent of the replicas like the Boxkite and Triplane, which could entertain the crowds more spectacularly. While the pilots at Old Warden were certainly interested to 'hop' the veterans, because no test pilot is able to resist flying something different, even for a few seconds, there is a world of difference between 'hopping' and making a full circuit.

So it was that when I was asked to 'hop' the Blackburn my primary concern was not to see if I could get as high as possible for as long as I could, but rather to ensure that I did not damage the oldest aeroplane in the Collection capable of real flight. It is a very different sensation climbing into a real veteran rather than a replica; one feels an enormous responsibility. One is aware of the attention of the mechanics who have spent long hours restoring this old aeroplane; they will not make adverse comment (they are too gentlemanly), but one cannot help feeling that this machine really belongs to them. One becomes intensely self-critical; any fumbling, any unnecessary burst of power, can produce a degree of self-recrimination worthy of any disciple of Chairman Mao!

There is no such thing as a quick familiarisation 'hop', with precious engine hours guarded so devotedly. Indeed, one is lucky to have the opportunity to run the engine at all before the display, so one hopes the crowd will be sympathetic towards any pilot who stops his engine in mid-field – rotary engine life is measured in minutes! The immediate problem I encountered was rather fundamental – how did I get in? Before I could phrase the question, a short wooden ladder appeared miraculously from nowhere. (Later I learned that it had been swiped from the Boxkite.) However, I consoled myself with the thought that there were plenty of natural footholds for an athletic pilot on that aeroplane!

Having narrowly avoided a rather nasty accident with a prominent rudder cable, I arrived at the cockpit area only to find that a solid-looking fuselage cross-member effectively prevented my getting into the pilot's chair. To my horror one of the mechanics gave it a sharp tug, whereupon it hinged upwards, allowing access to the seat. Once seated, with the cross-member clipped down, it acts as a safety bar, almost dispensing with the need to use the harness. However, being a firm believer in both belt and braces, I secured the Sutton harness. The geometry of the cockpit leaves much to be desired, as the pedals are too far away and are very close together, while the wheel, closely resembling the steering wheel of a sports car in both shape and location, moves in a completely foreign manner. Instead of moving in a fore-and-aft plane, the control column is attached to a pivot beneath the panel, with the result that when the elevators are up the wheel swings downwards until it practically touches the seat, while with full down elevator the wheel moves up until it obliterates all forward view. This vertical motion of the wheel takes quite a bit of getting used to. Ailerons of course are non-existent, but it is fascinating to operate the wing-warping and to see the large chord wing twisting with the able assistance of a conglomeration of pulleys and cables.

The instrument panel is painfully simple. There, in the centre, in solitary splendour, reposes a rev counter. That is it. No ASI, altimeter, or even oil pressure gauge, the latter, I suppose, being a bit superfluous on a rotary engine anyway, as the aviator can be in no doubt that oil is being supplied to the engine, if one is to judge by the amount of castor oil that usually drenches oneself. There is no windscreen, and the pilot sits practically 'on' rather than 'in' the fuselage, thus requiring warm and oilproof clothing even on a summer's day. Although the Blackburn is rather spartan in its accessories, it is at least liberally endowed with engine controls – there are five of them! There they sit, practically defying the aviator to find the right combination for starting. A large brass Victorian electric light switch has been pressed into service as a magneto switch, and there is an ignition cut-out (blip) button on the wheel. This latter can dispense some painful electric shocks to keep the aviator on his toes!

At first glance one is horrified to see what appears to be no fewer that three throttle levers, but a reassuring explanation is soon forthcoming. There is indeed a throttle, which works in theory only; subsequent experiment showed that although it did operate after a fashion, it also flooded the engine at low revs. The other two controls were the standard rotary engine air lever and fine adjustment lever. All of this for a tiny seven-cylinder 50hp engine!

Having satisfied myself that I was securely installed and that the primitive control system was likely to function to order, I passed the few minutes before starting in absorbing the appearance and attitude of the machine as it sat on the ground, for with no flight instruments this exercise was to be carried out literally by the seat of the pants. In spite of my preoccupation I was able from my vantage point to observe the staggering flight of the other two veterans with their tiny three-cylinder engines, and was pleased to note that they were not being affected by that terrible meteorological phenomenon, 'light turbulence'. Even the Blériot managed a hop of 50 yards. Now the Gnome was being primed, with neat petrol being injected into each tiny cylinder. I set the engine controls according to the briefing: throttle near full, air lever set to half, and petrol (fine adjustment) closed. The Gnome was pulled over with that wheezing 'clonk' peculiar to rotaries, and an invisible prop swinger shouted 'Contact'. The Victorian brass switch was selected on, and the prop was swung. The little engine instantly roared into life in a cloud of blue castor oil smoke as the priming fuel caught. I waited until this was exhausted, and when the engine cut out I

opened the fine adjustment, whereupon the Gnome picked up again and buzzed away merrily. Thirty seconds after starting, the engine was ready for take-off, for this is a dead loss oil system. I occupied this time by finding the positions of air lever and fine adjustment for full power and slow running, the only two realistic settings on a rotary engine. Full power gives a clean 1,200rpm, and it idles at 700 to 800.

I waved the chocks away and used the button to blip the engine as I taxied the few yards to the take-off point. I was concerned in case even in this short time the plugs might oil up, but the Gnome ran sweetly, just like a sewing machine. Two burly mechanics held the tail as I increased power to maximum, and as I dropped my hand they released their grip. The monoplane ran lightly across the grass, as I dabbed the rudder experimentally. It didn't seem to make much difference, so I left it alone. The aircraft ignored me completely and continued to run straight. I wondered how fast I was going

– it looked about fast enough to fly. I thought the tail was up but I couldn't really be sure – the confused slipstream with no windscreen ahead of me had destroyed my sense of feel. I tugged experimentally at the wheel – I couldn't move it! What was happening? I pulled even harder, with no result, then I remembered the wheel must come 'down' for the elevators to go up.

I tried this gently, and momentarily we were airborne; with no ASI I was afraid of stalling, and as I relaxed the pressure she sank back to earth. At least she was stable. I repeated the experiment, and this time I noted that she responded slowly to the lateral control. But now we were running out of field; the engine levers required me to stretch forward to reach them, so rather than unbalance the craft I held down the blip button, receiving a series of painful electric shocks in the process! The Blackburn sank gently to the ground, and at last I was able to reach the levers and release the confounded button. What a way to fly! I was covered with castor oil and my hand was still tingling. But for several seconds it really flew. There was no wind so I had the machine turned around for the return hop.

This time I held her just clear of the ground and found that she responded gently but correctly to the controls, but I was still having trouble with the elevator control system. But somehow, though she had not exceeded 10 feet of altitude for many years, I had the feeling that she had enough thrust and control to really fly.

I waited impatiently for the end of the display before approaching David Ogilvy, Shuttleworth's General Manager, with the idea: what an added attraction it would be if this old aeroplane could demonstrate 'full' flight. David at first hesitated, but then agreed that if the machine made two more hops and did not falter, I could take responsibility for the aircraft during a circuit. I know what that meant if anything went wrong – I should certainly have to flee the country! The engine again hummed sweetly as though eager to carry the machine into the air. The two hops were uneventful, except that I used every second to gain as much knowledge of the aeroplane as I could. Again the mechanics held me back as I carefully set the engine to full power, trying to listen for any change in note that might herald trouble, and sensitive to any possible variation. 1,200rpm, healthy and steady, and as I again dropped my hand the tail was released. Straight and true she rolled, accelerating gently, but this time, hopefully, she would not be made to stop. The engine beat strongly as we passed the point where she unstuck on the last run, but I let her roll, gathering speed, for I was afraid of getting on the wrong side of the drag curve. I pressed gently down on the wheel and she lifted off cleanly.

For a few seconds I held her parallel to the ground, noting carefully the nose position on the horizon, then I let her settle into the gentlest of climbs with the nose cowling apparently 1 inch above the horizon. The engine was as smooth as a turbine at 1,220rpm, and I decided that if I maintained this rpm with a healthy engine I must have reached the optimum condition for climbing. I was two-thirds down the field at about 30 feet. Now was the time to stop – or never. The machine was willing – now we were committed, but as I left the field behind me she was starting to sink; with mounting alarm I flew as carefully as I knew how, coaxing her, giving a little, taking a little. Down, down, now we were only 10 feet over the standing corn, the engine still pulling with all of its tiny heart. And slowly, very slowly, again we started to climb.

Now there was a new hazard – telephone wires ahead! I flew directly at them, with one eye on the rev counter – 1,240rpm; that must mean excess speed above normal climb speed. I lifted her over the wires, and dived a little to regain speed. Now there was open countryside ahead, and I concentrated

on gaining height before trying a turn back to the field. I knew that everyone on the field was deeply concerned, but I placed my trust in that sturdy little engine and kept climbing. Now for a turn – to the right would be best. I was now 200 or 300 feet up, so I could afford to lower the nose a little. The flat Bedfordshire countryside rotated steadily beyond the round aluminium cowling, and at last I was heading back towards the field. But now something else was wrong – the aircraft was shuddering – surely it couldn't be stalling? I lowered the nose and the shuddering got worse – what on earth was happening? Then I remembered my experiences with the Triplanes, which behaved in the same way when the controls were crossed. I checked – the rudder seemed more or less central, but I just could not tell by looking whether I was carrying any wing-warp.

'Just a minute, though – she does feel a little wing-heavy. The shuddering is worse – I don't like this'.

The left wing felt heavy so I pressed gentle right rudder. The shuddering disappeared, and so did the wing-heaviness. With such an exposed cockpit I just could not tell if I was sideslipping. Everything was slowly getting blurred as the castor oil spray settled on my goggles. In my struggles to get a handkerchief out of my pocket the machine reared up and I instinctively pushed on the wheel. Of course, nothing happened for long seconds until I remembered that I must lift the wheel to lower the nose. It was only 5 minutes since I took off, but it seemed like an hour. Everything was now running with castor oil, and I was sure that the oil deflector was not fitted when the machine was rebuilt. As I reached the field I estimated my height at 700 feet, every inch a struggle against drag and gravity. Now the monoplane seemed to have remembered how to fly, for I was not working so hard, and the turns were more coordinated. She curved gracefully in the sky, almost transparent with her clear-doped fabric showing her skeletal construction. So frail she looked from the ground, but high above the earth she felt a sturdy little machine, willing and responsive. I was amazed at her docility and gentle stability; was this an accident of design, or the product of a brilliant mind?

The light was going; we had to go down. I pulled back the fine adjustment and we glided easily in a gentle spiral; the nose was well down, and I had changed my grip on the wheel. By holding it with both hands together at the top I could control the machine with a normal push-pull action. As we came in over the woods in a steep controlled glide I realised with a little surprise that I had not consciously been concerned by the absence of an airspeed indicator. Somehow she felt right, and somehow I 'knew' that this was the right speed, without knowing what it actually was. With the fine adjustment closed, I let her settle and she touched delicately on three points as lightly as a feather – what a delightful old aeroplane! I caught the engine on the fine adjustment and taxied on the button, receiving another shock from the infernal thing.

Now the old Blackburn has entered another era of her experience, for, weather permitting, she will be able to fly properly at the Shuttleworth flying days, a wonderful historical exhibit, showing not only the achievement of a pioneer but, by comparison, the achievement of the intervening years.

The modern aeroplane, with all its sophistication, is, of course, much easier to fly. But I personally would not exchange all the comforts in the world for the pleasure and sheer thrill of flying a real veteran machine, especially when it is the oldest flying aeroplane in England.

14

*In Canada we were not allowed to impose any negative
'g', so of course, being students, we did.*

Harvard

WHEN it comes to selecting an advanced training aeroplane for military service, the basic concept is much the same now as it was thirty-six years ago – to obtain a low-cost trainer with the characteristics of a high-speed fighter. This was precisely the problem facing the North American design team in the mid-1930s, when the monoplane fighter with retractable undercarriage and variable-pitch propeller was beginning to make its presence felt. Initially the company produced a fixed-gear 'basic combat' aircraft, but the design quickly moved to a retractable undercarriage, and the North American Texan was born. The RAF ordered 400 machines, and to the disgust of many Americans promptly renamed it the 'Harvard'. In all, some 15,000 of these aircraft were built, and served in many countries. They presented a formidable challenge to students brought up on the gentle Tiger Moth, for not only were they complicated, but they were powerful, big and heavy. Evil tales surrounded the machine, although in retrospect they were probably initiated by hoary instructors with a twisted sense of humour and fostered by successive generations of demoralised students.

I first met the Harvard as a junior flight cadet in Canada, in the company of a dozen or so fellow Acting Pilot Officers of the RAF. At that time 30 per cent of the RAF students were trained under the Empire Air Scheme, which had its foundation in the dark days of the Second World War. They used Harvards then, too. Our station was RCAF Moose Jaw, which, being in the middle of the prairie, was surrounded by relatively flat and almost featureless scenery. When we got there the whole place was covered by snow, with the associated sub-zero temperatures of the Canadian winter. We were later to learn of the effects of temperature on the local speed of sound, but that day we had a practical demonstration as the school Harvards become airborne. In those temperatures, at 2,250rpm the propeller tips were well and truly sonic, and wave after wave of sound blared and battered between the hangars. It all contributed to our sense of anticipation and excitement: we were in the RAF and we were going to learn to fly!

The Harvard was originally an advanced trainer, so our consternation could be imagined when we found that this monster was to be used for ab initio training. One familiarisation ride and the game was on. I thought I had an advantage, namely 100 hours on club Tigers at home. How wrong I was! We all started right from the beginning and were required to solo in 21 hours. This seems a long time by present-day instructional standards, but it is perhaps an indication of the complexity of the aeroplane in its new role of basic trainer, and the mixture of awe and respect and, dare I suggest it, downright fright with which most of us approached the task. In fairness, most of the RAF contingent took between 10 and 14 hours to solo, but one foreign gentleman took 36 hours. The instructors had a hard time of it, as they had fourteen different nationalities to contend with and there was always the attendant language problem. One such instance was when a heavily accented voice was heard over the R/T to declare, 'I have an animal in my cockpit.' A request for further information produced the statement, 'I do not know the name of this animal but I do not like it.' The ensuing panic can be imagined – half the school fleet orbiting at 2,000 feet while our hero is lined up on straight-in approach about 10 miles out. After touchdown he cut his engine and rolled to a stop in the middle of the runway, to be instantly surrounded by fire trucks, ambulances, the CO and the duty officer brandishing a lethal-looking revolver. The 'animal' in question turned out to be a harmless 4-inch locust!

One of the first things we had to become familiar with was the starting ritual, since all the engine starting controls were in the front cockpit. Our Mark II aircraft had a starter pedal located between the rudder pedals, and with the requirement to hand pump to maintain fuel pressure, catch the engine on the throttle, hold the stick back and operate the starter in a manner similar to the racing driver's heel/toe action, one distinctly felt the need for a couple of spare hands. This inertia starter was a rather cunning device; with the pedal in one position it gradually accelerated a flywheel for some 12 to 15 seconds, and when reversed it disconnected the electric motor and engaged the flywheel with the engine through a clutch, allowing the stored-up energy to rotate the engine. Although primitive, it was remarkably efficient. The flywheel could also be wound up externally by a sweating and cursing mechanic, who performed his function in close proximity to the propeller. It looked extremely dangerous, although I never heard of anyone getting a haircut.

Taxiing the aeroplane was slightly unnerving, because to carry out short-radius turns one had to push the stick fully forward (to withdraw the tailwheel

lock), then jab one brake to start the turn, all of this with an appreciable amount of power. The school ruling was that we taxied on the brakes and therefore had to hold the rudder control while we operated the toe brakes. This produced pilots with extremely flexible ankles, but was of little benefit otherwise.

Describing take-off, the Pilot's Notes state that there is a slight tendency to swing to the left. Although I agree that this statement is correct, as students we questioned the definition of the word 'slight'. The key to this is perhaps in the next paragraph, which states that the throttle must be opened carefully. Certainly if you banged the throttle open the rudder work had to be exactly right. Acceleration was not particularly high, and the aircraft pounded along the runway for an appreciable time before unstick. Once the tail came up the view was good and there were no real problems. There was always sufficient rudder to contain any swing problem on take-off; perhaps we students got into trouble by simply not applying enough rudder, or by having the pedals incorrectly adjusted. Pilot's Notes advice to apply full right rudder trim prior to take-off was not necessary and, by its apparent association with Spitfire trim settings, could almost have promoted a swing by auto-suggestion.

On the Harvard II one had to remember to select the power push lever during the undercarriage retraction process, otherwise the boots would hang down while the aircraft disappeared into the distance. This power push merely activated the hydraulic circuit for operation of service, so that the system was not subjected to full pressure all the time.

In flight the aircraft has the feel of a heavy high-performance piston-engined machine, but additionally has its own lively feel. It was an excellent machine for learning formation flying, and yet it was not so stable that it wouldn't fly decent aerobatics. In Canada we were not allowed to impose any negative 'g', so of course, being students, we did. The result of this was that the engine coughed and picked up again with an ear-splitting roar as it momentarily oversped. We never got away with anything because in addition the aeroplane became covered with oil in the process. Cleaning oil-covered Harvards can be quite a deterrent against inverted flying!

It was in the regime of stalling, spinning and aerobatics that the Harvard really made pilots out of airframe drivers. There was a certain amount of buffeting before the stall, but the 'g' break when it came was very sudden. The aircraft would drop a wing, especially with flaps down, and if the stick was held back it would spin. In a tight turn the stall would come without any warning (other than slight buffet). The result of this was a very fast flick-roll to the right, which in a left-hand turn left a slightly surprised pilot straight and level, but in a right turn it invariably flicked on to its back. It was often demonstrated by the instructors that it was quicker to continue rolling right to erect rather than to try and stop the whole thing and then reverse it.

Spinning a Harvard is a complete story on its own. Prior to spinning one must ensure both hoods are closed to avoid losing panels due to suction. Also one set 2,000rpm, 14 inches of manifold pressure, then put the ICO to cut-off, which cut off all fuel to the engine. This was to prevent flooding the intake with fuel with the attendant fire risk. In particular the rpm lever was emphatically not to be moved to the maximum rpm position during spinning, because the increased rpm could give recovery problems due to the gyroscopic effects, and also because of the risk of overspeeding in the pull-out.

The first two turns of the spin are oscillatory and are accompanied by considerable buffeting and control column snatching. As the spin settles down the buffeting and snatching become less, but the spin is generally unpleasant. Normal recovery action is effective, but the rotation speeds up for 1½ turns before the spin stops. During the pull-out the mixture is selected back to rich and the engine picks up, often with a loud bang.

Much has been written about the evils of spinning a Harvard. As students, in blissful ignorance, we used to carry out spins and recoveries under the hood as part of our instrument training. One thing all this did for us was that it taught us not to be afraid of the aeroplane and to be able to handle any situation with confidence. How many pilots these days know how to interpret a turn and slip indicator in a spin?

In a Harvard, aerobatics were a joy. It took time to build up speed in a dive, but once the speed was there the manoeuvres followed each other with ease and precision. One could never be rough with a Harvard; a little too tight over the top of a loop and the horizon blurred as the aircraft flick-rolled in protest. Flicks were inevitably forbidden, but obviously nobody had told the aeroplane as it would auto-rotate at the slightest provocation. As one got to know the aircraft one could perhaps wish for a little more power, but this is true of every aerobatic aeroplane I have flown – an aerobatic pilot is never satisfied! The Harvard is the only aeroplane I know where one can stall the ailerons with too vigorous an application; this is most noticeable in the vertical roll. To achieve the maximum number of vertical rolls one must apply aileron smoothly instead of banging them hard over.

Even in my early training days I was keen on aerobatics, and a large percentage of my basic training course was devoted to the subject, to the detriment, I regret to say, of more mundane subjects such as navigation and map-reading exercises. So it was that I thought I knew what aerobatics were all about by the time I reached wings standard. Earlier this year I had the opportunity to fly Patrick Lindsay's Harvard G-BAFM, and to display it on his behalf. In the intervening period the advent of the Zlin had taught me a thing or two about aerobatics, so that when I flew Patrick's aeroplane I began to realise that in Canada I had barely been on nodding terms with the Harvard. Manoeuvres that I had never seen at that time were well within the machine's capabilities. But perhaps the most interesting thing was that all the manoeuvres could be flown more gently and accurately than had been the case in the past. The Harvard, it would seem, can always teach something of value.

If the aircraft had any problems at all from the students' point of view, it was the landing. A glide approach with full flap required 90mph over the hedge, and in fact, if one can land a Tiger Moth, all one needs in the Harvard is a firm, confident touch. Most of our student landing accidents were due to indecision either as to the correct technique or as to the decision to go round again. The only landing accident I saw that was due to overconfidence was a Turkish officer who came sailing down finals with his gear firmly locked up. Red lights, red Verys, and exhortations to overshoot produced no reaction. Finally, with the controller practically screaming at him, he elected to reply, 'I am the captain of this aeroplane, and my wheels are down.' In fact, all it needed was a new propeller, a quick retraction test, and an instructor flew it back to base otherwise undamaged – a tough aeroplane, the Harvard.

The Harvard had a rather unfriendly tendency to drop a wing, particularly if the hold-off was high or if the stick was pulled back quickly. However, this was where the earlier stalling and spinning experience paid off; one used the rudder to contain a wing drop, and this ingrained habit was to ease conversion to more powerful tailwheel aircraft in later years. 'The landing is never over until the aircraft has stopped', and this is especially true of the Harvard. But it kept us literally on our toes, and we were never afraid to use engine, rudder and brake all at the same time if necessary.

We flew about 200 hours each on the Harvard in training. I suppose that in retrospect one always has a soft spot for the aircraft on which one learned to fly, but this aircraft was something rather special. We flew long solo cross-countries at night, with the hood open and the aircraft trimmed out with the big Pratt & Whitney purring away. Some of us missed the turning point and flew across the border into the USA, where we were intercepted by keen P-51 pilots who sat on our wingtips trying to pick out our identification. If this happened, the drill was to gradually decelerate until the P-51 stalled and vanished into the darkness.

With the coming of winter the oil dilution system of the Harvard was put to good use, and we had to strap in inside the heated hangar. As soon as we were towed out we had to start up before frozen oil and fingers required aircraft and crew to be returned to the hangar to thaw out. The course was well-organised, so that in the winter we flew instruments. This meant that the student sat in the rear seat under the hood, and, incidentally, on top of the heater outlet! This did not endear us to our instructors!

We listened to the dots and dashes of the radio range let-down system until our ears rang. (This was an archaic and long-winded system but was very good for training.) When we could stand it no more we were given 5 minutes' rest from this task while the instructor thawed out his frozen limbs by aerobatting or dog-fighting with a similarly frozen colleague. The instructor's advice was concise: 'Keep your head on a swivel and your eyeballs uncaged.' He applied it to air fighting, but in these days of congested airspace it holds good for every phase of flight.

We learned a lot at FTS. Perhaps more in that short period than we would ever do again in a similar period. It was a good school, and it taught us, comparatively speaking, to university standards. It could not have been done as well with another aeroplane. A good trainer, the Harvard.

15

Nobody knows how he got a T-33 out of the hangar, on a winter's night all by himself, got in, wearing only pyjamas, started up and took off on the short runway...

Snow Birds

WINTER in Europe brings the usual crop of cold weather problems, which always seem to catch us unprepared. We are surprised to hear lumps of ice clang on the fuselage, impelled by the rotation of the propellers, and we are often alarmed at the ensuing out-of-balance vibration. The CAA information circulars prophesy disaster if we do not ensure the wings are clear of frost and ice, to say nothing of turning and braking performance on ice-covered runways. We gravely learn of the maximum permitted depth of soft snow or slush for take-off, especially with a nosewheel undercarriage, and one has visions of pilots rushing about all over the runway with depth gauges.

If one is to judge by the number of bulletins and circulars, the lethal potential of ice and snow seems to be on the increase, yet with every passing year our knowledge of winter operations gets better. But still we seem to be unprepared and every year brings a new toll of those who are caught out.

Before all-through jet training became commonplace, pilots in various air forces started out on pistons, and converted to jets half-way through the flying course. Now this was quite a shaker for many young pilots, quite a few of whom got no further. On top of the usual problems was the fact that when we left our sedate old Harvards and moved on to the sleek T-33 Silver Star, winter had the training base firmly in its grip. This was not the rather

... winter had the training base firmly in its grip.

miserable winter of Europe, but the fierce, lethal Arctic conditions of the Canadian Prairies, where temperatures often reached 40 degrees below zero.

We could scarcely believe that anybody could do anything in those temperatures, for we had to scuttle rapidly from building to building on our route between the mess and the hangar, pausing to recover each time from that stunning cold. All the buildings, including the hangars, were heated, and we used to do our pre-flight inspections inside when the weather was really cold, strapping in and being towed outside just before start-up.

On other days, when the sun shone, and protected as we were wearing our heavy flying gear, we operated from the tarmac in front of the hangars, much as normal. On a few occasions we were reminded of the Arctic conditions by such problems as the nosewheel on the T-33, which was free-castoring, and which could turn through 90 degrees quite easily, whereupon the only way to straighten it was to increase power and hope to get some traction.

On this particular day one of our young heroes had managed to 'cock' his nosewheel right on the flight line in front of the hangar, and soon every window contained its quota of faces eager to see the fun.

We had not long to wait. A newly joined airman, impressed by all this sound and fury as our colleague struggled to blast his way out of his predicament, stopped, and in spite of the cold, stood there transfixed. The point of friction on packed snow was reached and surpassed just as the throttle was opened wide in desperation.

The T-33 shot straight across the tarmac, nosewheel still cocked at 90 degrees, the jet blast lifting large lumps of hard-packed snow, flinging them high into the air like a gargantuan blizzard. It also lifted the airman, who took off through space like a large black snowflake, spinning end over end until he disappeared behind Air Traffic together with the rest of the debris.

In fact, he wasn't much hurt, but the Flight Commander took the opportunity to point out the dangers of using high power in dispersal, and nobody needed reminding about the effects of jet blast, especially 'Snow-plough Charlie', as we immediately christened our crestfallen colleague.

Not all these winter hazards were as obvious as that one. One day, having done a dual trip, I was scheduled to fly a solo exercise after the aircraft had been refuelled. It was an especially cold day, but according to the wind chill chart we were not yet down to the point where a hangar changeover was necessary. Ninety wind chill units was the equivalent of a warm summer's day, while at 1400 exposed flesh froze.

We were operating at 1800 that day, so I was not hanging about doing my external check. As a result I missed one little switch in the rear cockpit – the master speedbrake switch. Having got my mask and helmet on, canopy closed and engine started, I soon found the problem. I had to open the canopy and remove my mask to shout to one of the groundcrew and get him to close the switch, but in this short time the inlet valve on my oxygen mask froze solid!

With those old A.13 masks, if the inlet valve froze it prevented exhalation, so I taxied to the take-off point making noises over the R/T like a drowning walrus. My idea was to get airborne and stay at low level using high power and full cockpit heat to thaw things out.

This was fine except in no time at all I was hurtling up Lake Manitoba at nought feet well on the way to the T-33 speed record, still scarcely able to breathe.

I should soon be inside the Arctic Circle itself at this rate, so I decided to orbit. This was even more strenuous, as the speed took some time to come off by pulling 'g' and I needed full power to keep the heat in the cockpit. Finally the 'g' did it, and with a bang and a whoosh the valve freed. By this time I was fairly whacked, and as I had used up most of my fuel by tearing around at low level. I thought I'd better go home, which I did. Bit of a waste of time, that was, really.

The T-33 had one collector fuel tank into which all other tanks were emptied by electric booster pumps, from which it then flowed to the engine. One had to keep one's eyes on the level of this vitally important tank, and to help this a red low-level warning light was fitted to the panel of both cockpits.

One fine morning an instructor and pupil were up doing some forced-landing practice, and the student was not doing too well. He was concentrating so hard that he had forgotten his fuel drill and didn't even notice the red warning light.

The instructor had decided to see how far he would go before he changed tanks, but as the aircraft got lower and things started to get out of hand even the instructor forgot it, so that when he finally had to take control and overshoot, the tank was nearly empty.

The wheels and flaps locked up and the clean aircraft started to accelerate away from the field with the instructor swearing fluently at the student (it was different in those days!), when the engine flamed out.

Now a clean T-33 is a very efficient flying machine and the instructor managed to get in five (all unsuccessful) relight attempts before the aircraft reached the ground, some 5 miles further on. Manitoba is quite a flat province – prairie country – so there was nothing much to impede progress. They jettisoned the canopy, which did little to slow them, but really let in the winter air with a vengeance.

It must have been the wildest toboggan ride of them all – the T-33 bounced and ricocheted for miles before it finally slid to a stop – those big tip tanks made excellent outriggers. When it did stop it shoved its nose under a barbed wire fence, and the wire ran up to the top of the windscreen arch, where, precariously, it stopped.

They sat rigid, unable to move in case the wire came down like a guillotine. By the time the rescue party got there they were practically frozen stiff – but the instructor hadn't stopped swearing!

The strangest tale of all was that of the so-called 'Pyjama Pilot', in which the CO had ordered one of his inebriated officers to retire to his quarters during the course of a mess evening, and this worthy had then decided it was a nice evening for a flip.

Nobody knows how he got a T-33 out of the hangar, on a winter's night all by himself, got in, wearing only pyjamas, started up and took off on the short runway, which we only used for Otters and the like.

There were no lights anywhere on the field, and since the telephone wires across the runway were still intact we supposed he must have gone under them! The flight only lasted 2 minutes, before he pranged it just outside the aerodrome, and the first thing anyone knew was when this bedraggled, bloodstained pyjama-clad figure staggered into the guardroom an hour later.

It was impossible to get a T-33 off that runway even in daytime – nobody could survive a crash and an hour's exposure clad only in pyjamas – but he did. Somebody must really look after young fighter pilots!

16

On and on we flew, not knowing if we were over land or water, not knowing what instruments to trust, while I put out a series of emergency calls.

A Night to Remember

EVERY now and then, in the best-regulated circles, something happens to spoil the smooth pattern of events. When this occurrence is related to the persistent malfunction of a piece of machinery, one has to resist the temptation to bestow intelligence or even low bestial cunning on an inert and complex assembly of components. With a motor car, one vents one's wrath on the manufacturer's representative or on the garage, but with ships, perhaps because of their individual personalities, one succumbs to the belief that now and then a particular vessel has a jinx on it, and the reputation of an unhappy ship spreads far and wide. Even in these sophisticated days we cannot escape.

Aircraft, too, have personalities, and pilots are well aware of this feeling between man and machine, especially when flying at great heights over vast and unoccupied regions of the world. An aircraft is more potentially lethal to its occupants than is a sea-going vessel, so perhaps that is why we say that while a ship may be 'jinxed', a certain aircraft may exhibit the behaviour of a mad bull elephant expelled from the herd. They share a common name – rogue.

This is the story of a few hours spent at night in the company of such a rogue. Shining in the sun on the tarmac at Nairobi, it looked just like any other photo-reconnaissance Canberra – sky-blue beneath, camouflaged on top, its camera ports open, staring wide-eyed, its bomb bay half-filled by a long-range fuel tank. Like the other machines on the squadron it could carry more than its own weight in fuel, and could fly for great distances at high altitudes.

But it was different in one respect: constructed at about the same time as the other machines, it had flown only a quarter of the hours, and was therefore relatively new – a good aircraft for a young squadron pilot, one might think. But the reason why it had low hours was that it was continually giving trouble – nothing really serious, at least not yet.

The sun was setting as we walked out to the aircraft. This was to be merely a positioning flight from Nairobi to Aden, about 2½ hours flying. We had all the modern navigational aids at that time, including the then secret Doppler equipment that is now used on modern commercial jets. We were relatively light

as we were carrying fuel in the fuselage only – this would give us 2 hours reserve fuel. I checked the form F.700, which showed the aircraft to be serviceable, some work on the Air Mileage Unit and the radio compass having been carried out.

As the navigator checked his gear, I punched the starter buttons and the Avons shrieked into life. Flaps, bomb doors, camera doors, airbrakes all checked with the groundcrew, I waved the chocks away. Our third crew member sat on the folding seat, for there were only two ejection seats in the photo-recce Canberra. Although we were lightly laden, I stabilised at full power on the brakes before starting the take-off; Nairobi is nearly 5,500 feet above sea level!

Slowly we gathered speed, and now we had left the tarmac and were thundering along the hard dirt runway, leaving a colossal trail of red dust. I eased back the stick as we reached 130 knots, and with the gear retracting we flashed across the trees at the end of the runway, turned onto course and settled into the climb. As we passed through 20,000 feet the controller told us we were clear to leave his frequency and that he was now closing the airfield.

We bid each other goodnight, and as I saw the black arc of night sweeping up over the sky like a gigantic blackout curtain, my navigator told me that he could not tune the radio compass to the beacon at Garissa.

If this was a warning, it passed unheeded, because we knew that with the coming of night the radio compass would not be reliable for another hour, and anyway the Doppler appeared to be working well, showing us to be on track. Lulled by the low hum of the engines, we climbed on into the stratosphere.

Soon we levelled at cruise altitude, and I started to trim the aircraft, but I found that I had to keep adjusting the lateral trim. I was almost certain that we were turning very gently, but both main and standby compasses showed a steady heading. I put the feeling down to the fact that the curved mantle of darkness was causing an optical illusion; I concentrated on flying the aircraft on instruments, for there was nothing to see outside.

With no autopilot, my attention remained in the cockpit, and I tried to keep a mental dead reckoning picture of our progress; soon it would be time to give Aden a call, but with only VHF we would have to be within 100 miles before they would hear us.

Suddenly my attention was caught by an unearthly flickering blue light: I looked up, enthralled, to see a weird display of St Elmo's fire dancing across the windscreen. The two crew members stirred and the intercom came to life after almost an hour of silence, for the cockpit of a high-flying jet is peaceful.

Intrigued with the wild splendour of the display, I suddenly noticed that I had wandered off heading a few degrees. I must pay attention! The phenomenon of electrical discharge was caused by the fact that we had entered a belt of cirro-stratus cloud, and now that night had truly fallen the sky outside was as black as ink. 'You should get them now,' said the navigator, but my R/T call produced no reply. I turned up the volume and the crackling became louder – that was all. 'The Doppler shows 20 miles to go,' said the navigator. Still nothing. We cruised on in silence.

Well, there was nothing for it but to go down and look. I eased back on the throttles and the altimeter started to unwind. At 30,000 feet we came out of cloud, but there was no sign of an airfield or a town, indeed of anything at all, save for tiny pinpoints of light far below. 'We're now 15 minutes beyond ETA,' I reminded the navigator, 15 minutes representing a very long way at 500mph. Try as we might we could not identify the tiny lights – were they desert camp-fires or fishing vessels? I levelled out at 14,000 feet – the mountains of the Hadramhaut are 11,000 feet high. We flew on, the Doppler showing that we must be heading up towards Yemen, the navigator checking and re-checking his calculations, but there was no apparent mistake. Finally we had to turn south, in the hope of seeing a coastline – the lights must be the desert camp-fires of the nomadic tribes.

On and on we flew, reluctant to climb lest we miss the coastline, yet aware of the high consumption of precious fuel at this low altitude. The radio compass swung aimlessly in circles, and then I saw that the main compass was 40 degrees different from the standby – which was correct?

The high cirrus cloud obscured the sky, so we could not use the sextant, nor even get a rough bearing on a star. If the main compass was wrong, then both the Ground Position Indicator and the Doppler would give us false information, because they received their data from the main compass. On and on we flew, not knowing if we were over land or water, not knowing what instruments to trust, while I put out a series of emergency calls.

How I wished I had started with the wing tanks full. Then, very faintly, I heard a voice. It was the D/F homer at Aden. I asked for a course to steer and very faintly I heard '140 degrees'. This was incredible – how could we be north-west of Aden? At any rate, on a southerly heading we were going in the right general direction. I asked the controller whether he was giving us a 'course to steer', or a bearing, but the reply was unintelligible. I pressed the transmit button four times, to signify that I wanted a course to steer, but the controller's voice, very faint now, said that our transmissions were intermittent!

What we didn't know then was that the airman on duty was only allowed to pass true bearings – and not to give any other information unless his commanding officer was present. The transmissions faded out, and on that clue we assumed that the '140 degrees' had indeed been a true bearing and that we were far out over the Gulf of Aden, heading for the Indian Ocean!

The interference on the radio was diabolical as I turned onto a northerly heading and started to climb, all the time transmitting for a steer.

At 26,000 feet I closed down one engine; five tanks were now dry and we were running on the last. Slowly we sank lower as I flew at our best range speed, then through the static I heard a new voice, confident and capable – the airman had at last summoned his CO. 'Steer 330 degrees for Aden' – the instructions could just be heard. We still had no idea of our range – in 15 minutes I would have to give the order to bale out – but into what? Land or sea? And the sea was inhabited by sharks – not much hope there. I decided to wait until the engine actually flamed out before I would give the order – and the third crewman would have to fight his way out manually before the navigator ejected. The controller was coming in stronger now, but we were obviously not approaching in a straight line – the standby compass seemed nearly right, so I started to use that.

Then I saw it: a flashing light in the distance, flashing the code of the aerodrome. Could we make it? I throttled back and started to glide, and slowly the airfield and runway lights came into view. I relit the other engine as I joined the circuit, but left both throttled back as I dropped wheels and flaps and touched down – more than 4½ hours after take-off, with not enough fuel left for even one circuit. What had gone wrong? The work on the radio compass and Air Mileage Unit had been signed up, but not actually done. The Doppler and Ground Position Indicator had received false information from the compass, which in turn had failed because of arcing at high altitude, and the standby compass had failed by the same amount due to the electrical potential of the cloud that caused the St Elmo's fire.

The radio simply had a cracked plug through a pressure bulkhead. All this I was told later when the technical experts had finished their investigation. But why had the controller left his post for so long that evening? And when he scrambled the rescue organisation, why was the duty Shackleton in the middle of an engine change, and the Air Sea Rescue launch in dry dock for repairs? Why did all those things happen at the same time, when the situation was just right for disaster?

It was as though the aircraft really did have a personality, like a rogue elephant that tries to destroy everything, even itself in the end. Rubbish, you will say, of course no such thing can happen. The aircraft was carefully serviced, air-tested and pronounced 100 per cent serviceable, so my navigator and I took off for a training sortie in it. The hydraulic system failed completely and we were faced with a belly landing without flaps and airbrakes. She hit the ground hard and skidded down the runway in a shower of sparks and with a scream of tortured metal. We scrambled out and looked back at her, one wing resting on the ground, the other pointing at the sky like an accusing finger. Broken and torn, we could feel no sympathy for her. She was, after all, a rogue.

17

...there was now nobody in charge of the aeroplane as it wallowed drunkenly about the sky, the cockpit full of flying fists.

Across the Iron Curtain

WITH the return of the British Aerobatic Team from Kiev after the Eighth World Aerobatic Championships, it is interesting to look back ten years to when the contest was held in Moscow. This was the first time since well before the war that civil light aeroplanes were allowed to fly across Russia, but it was not the distance nor the weather factor that concerned us, for it was high summer, and the highest point en route was no more than 150 feet in a distance of 1,500 miles. Two things only worried us: the political situation, with all that this implied (I was serving in the RAF), and the quality of the fuel that we could expect. We had heard that only the Russian engines in the Yak 18s would perform properly on the very low grade of petrol we understood would be allocated to us, and this was of some concern, because at that time we were flying a Zlin 226, and with our relative inexperience in competition flying we needed all the permitted height plus continuous full power to complete the sequence in the relatively cool air of the UK. What would happen in Moscow in the full heat of summer if our engine was down on power?

As the departure time drew near, the team was invited to a cocktail party at the residence of the Soviet air attaché. This caused me an immediate panic, but the RAF security people thought I had better go, rather than risk an incident. 'But,' they said, 'watch what you drink and what you say!'

Dutifully we all assembled, and were much relieved to be offered fruit juice and talk on inconsequential matters. Then the air attaché came in and welcomed us, asking me how much flying I was doing. 'About one or two hours a week,' said I, thinking of aerobatic training. 'No,' he said, 'I mean at Farnborough, where you work!' I practically choked over my orange juice.

'Good heavens,' I said, looking at my watch, 'is that the time? We must be going!'

If this sort of thing could happen in London, what was going to happen in Moscow? By this time I was many times more concerned about the security situation than about the contest, but in fact nothing more untoward happened at all, even in Moscow, although we had plenty of problems in other areas.

We set off on a bright summer's morning in grand style, the Zlin leading, with a couple of long-suffering Tiger Club Stampes neatly tucked in, a formation that we were scarcely to break until we reached Moscow. Off to one side cruised our Jodel baggage aircraft, heavily weighed down with all our kit and spares. As one of our party remarked, all that was missing apart from a cat and a hot water bottle was about 12 knots!

Our journey started smoothly and easily, and we even had communication in the shape of battery-powered portable radios with which we could speak to the Jodel, which in turn was the master radio station for the formation. Flying

over the Low Countries, we were soon avoiding great towering masses of cloud as the afternoon cumulonimbus build-ups appeared. The Jodel stayed on track, straying closer to the menacing black clouds, while I led the formation away to the north, over the cooler coastal regions. After a lot of static, I could faintly hear the Jodel asking us if we were still airborne, which made us wonder what sort of weather he had run into. In fact, we stayed clear of the rough stuff and arrived at Wilhelmshaven 20 minutes ahead of him! Here we landed to refuel, but to our surprise not a soul was to be found! Eventually we ran the entire airport staff to earth; they were watching the World Cup on television, England versus Germany, and coincident with the arrival of the British Team came England's resounding victory in the Cup! I have never seen such a sour-faced lot as the fuel attendants who replenished our tanks!

With great relief we got airborne again, and after a smooth flight and a night-stop at Kiel, where we had the interesting experience of being served dinner in completely the reverse order, finishing with soup, we eventually reached Bornholm in the Baltic, the last western airfield before venturing into Communist airspace. Here we searched in vain for hangar space. I insisted that on no account was the Zlin going to stay outside overnight, in spite of opposition from some of the team, who were hot, tired and dusty, and wanted to get to the hotel. Finally we found a farm shed on the edge of the airport full of rusty machinery, old cars, etc, and anyway the door was too small. We emptied this and actually had to lift the Zlin and carry it in – there was no room to manoeuvre it! We also, impossibly, got a Stampe in too!

Next day we lost a good hour reversing this process, especially as we had to put all the rusty machinery back as well! Eventually we got airborne and were soon cruising in smooth air above the glittering waters of the Baltic towards Poland. By now the battery radios had all given up the ghost, which suited me because after the farm shed episode nobody was talking to me anyway! This was our longest leg, maximum endurance for the Stampes, and with no clear idea where the destination airfield was! We had been given an ADF frequency for the beacon at destination, but we had been unable to get a reliable geographical fix for the airfield. We knew it was near the town of Grudsiatz, and had decided if necessary to put down in any good field – only possible with our solid-tailwheel undercarriages.

In fact, we had no trouble finding the field, rough though it was, because of the dozens of gliders strewn about everywhere. Here we received a curious blend of Polish hospitality and Communist doctrine. We were not allowed to pay for anything, fuel included, and when we tried to give some money to the local children this was refused because they 'were well provided for'!

Our next stop was Allenstein, which used to be in Prussia, and here we were received enthusiastically, to the point where we were practically dragged into the local town to be the guests of honour at a 'dinner'. Plain fare it might have been, but to our hosts it was obviously the best they had to offer. Back at the airfield our aircraft had been refuelled with great care, and we were given a most friendly send-off on this leg into Russia. Polish petrol seemed to suit our engines, and we cruised at 85 knots to keep oil consumption down on the Stampes. One thing was certain – we were not going to risk mixing unknown oil in our engines, and we had little room to spare on board for spare tins. Every now and then I had to open up the Zlin to full power for a few seconds, because with its efficient propeller the rpm was so low that the plugs were beginning to foul.

Then we saw it, stretching from horizon to horizon as far as the eye could see – the Russian border. It consisted of a large wire fence, interspersed with look-out towers and bounded on each side by a ploughed strip of land, apparently running unbroken from the Black Sea to the Baltic! Now we really felt that we were penetrating into forbidden airspace, and in spite of our flight plan we instinctively closed up as if for mutual protection. Dramatically the countryside had changed from the well-tended cultivation of Poland to a bleak, drab, unending landscape, broken only by a solitary road seemingly without beginning or end. We felt a sense of depression as we stared about us in awe at this vast land containing nothing.

But if the land was empty, the sky was not. Within minutes of our crossing of the border, a silver swept-wing fighter, a MiG19, exploded upon us, flashing by with a crack and a roar only a few hundred feet away! Feeling utterly helpless, we watched it pull up and turn back for another look, while two more fighters roared past. They were obviously controlled by radar, but from where? Our charts showed no towns or airfields anywhere near. This was a dramatic demonstration of low-level radar coverage, for we knew from experience at home what poor radar returns our small machines offered. We sat, tensed, waiting for the next onslaught, but nothing came, as if the exercise was complete; the big stick had been waved at us!

We joined the circuit at Vilnius an hour later, but in complete contrast nobody took the slightest notice of us. Even when we taxied in and parked alongside some Polish team Zlins, no one paid us the slightest attention, as if

brightly painted western aeroplanes landed every day! The reason soon
became clear; we had arrived a day too soon, and no arrangements had been
made to receive us! Eventually we found someone who could speak English
and a hotel was arranged. There was no chance of hangarage, not even in a
farm shed, so we asked for fuel to be provided to fill the tanks before
overnight parking. (The Zlin had no drain tap in the fuel system to allow
water formed by condensation to be vented.) At about 7.00pm we met our
interpreter and put this request to him, but he was told that there would not
be any fuel until the morning. We insisted, and off he went again, only to be
told that the bowser driver had gone home! To cut a long story short, at
3.00am we still had no petrol, we had heard twenty-five different excuses, the
interpreter was asleep on his feet, and James Black and I were taking it in
turns to demand fuel and to doze for a few minutes! By now we reckoned
that if condensation was going to form, it would have done it, so we retired
to the hotel, incurring the displeasure of the staff by waking everybody up at
4.00am. Two hours' sleep and we were up again, this time to be driven to the
airport and paraded in a line in front of the main terminal. With sinister
thoughts of firing squads, we awaited developments.

Soon a bus drove up, and out poured a couple of dozen schoolchildren
armed with bouquets of flowers, which they proceeded to present to us.
Today was obviously arrival day, and this was the welcoming committee!
'Now,' they said, 'would you like some petrol?'

From here we became part of a giant aerial convoy, led by an Antonov
AN-2, a massive biplane with a 1,000hp engine, which wended its way
across Russia with the aerobatic machines in formation. For this purpose
we were all summoned to a briefing, where we were introduced to a small
rotund Russian with an unpronounceable name, who was the commander
of our 'group'. We were allocated various positions to fly in relation to the
'Big Ant', as we came to call it.

The briefing was conducted with the utmost seriousness. 'First, Antonov
– second Meester Carter.' (This was Nick in the Jodel D.140, our long-
suffering baggage aeroplane. For the rest of his days he will be 'Meester
Carter' to the British contingent.) 'Next troika' – the Soviet term for our 'vic'
of three aerobatic machines. Behind us came the three Polish Zlins, their
Aero 145 baggage aeroplane, and finally, at the rear, the sinister shape of a
Yak-18 two-seater – the whipper-in, whose task it was to see that nobody
strayed from the formation.

It was explained to us that the first leg was to be as far as Minsk, where the Antonov would fly into wind above the active runway and rock its wings, the language problem in flight being avoided by the complete absence of R/T amongst the acrobatic aeroplanes. This signal would require Nick to break away and land, followed by the Antonov, our 'troika' and so on, with the Yak-18 circling like a hawk above a mousehole until we were all down.

Finally the big moment came, and engines were started, all except one stubborn Gipsy in one of the Stampes, which obviously had decided that it wanted to go home, and not any deeper into Russia. Eventually it succumbed to the usual sharp blow below the impulse magneto, and we were all in business. No sooner had we started to taxi, however, than there were frantic signals to shut down. We never did discover what for.

Immediately we were given a second, and identical, briefing, whereupon we once again started up, and almost immediately had to shut down again. Yet a third briefing, again identical, and once more we started up, the now warm Gipsy really giving trouble this time. We assumed by all this that if the slightest hitch occurred in the operation, our perspiring commander was destined for the salt mines!

This time we actually got airborne, and it was with faint surprise that I saw this strange formation actually assembling in the planned order.

We had asked the Antonov pilot to keep the speed down to 150km/h, which would allow the Gipsies in the Stampes to run at 2,100rpm, thus preventing excessive consumption. However, at this speed the heavily laden Jodel was on the back side of the drag curve, which produced a definite tendency to wallow. In order to improve the situation it was decided to lighten the Jodel by allowing the spare pilot to ride in the Antonov, and by organising a rota system we arranged that each of us in turn would get a flight in this ancient and interesting machine. James was the first to fly in the Antonov, and little did he know what was in store!

Like an outsize bumble bee, the 'Big Ant' laboured heavily along, its olive green and red star rich against the dull and featureless background of the Russian steppes. Beyond was the Jodel, looking much happier at its lighter weight. We three, in a tight vic, were tucked in close to the Antonov's starboard wings, our close formation flying a source of comment to the Russian commercial crews, who obviously do not have any formation experience.

After a while I noticed the speed beginning to increase, causing anxiety to the two Stampe pilots. I signalled a change into echelon starboard and slid right up close to the Antonov, so that I could look into the cockpit. This manoeuvre did not go unnoticed by the Russian pilot, who became rather agitated by the close proximity of so many aeroplanes. I signalled 'slow down', which of course he did not understand. Luckily, James, peering out of the window, realised what was happening and by hand signals made the commander understand what was wanted. This was relayed volubly to the pilot, who was clutching the control wheel as though his life depended on it; I could see his white knuckles from the Zlin cockpit. The Antonov slowed down, and we reformed vic, to the obvious relief of the Russian crew, who were plainly unnerved by all this.

At 150 km/h everyone was relaxed and we droned on for mile after mile. At last Minsk appeared and, as briefed, the armada trundled majestically along the main Minsk runway. Half-way across the field, and still no wing rock from the Antonov. The commander's face could be seen moving from window to window, anxiety writ large upon his countenance.

Finally he turned to James and with despairing gestures indicated that we were all supposed to land. Fortunately James had attended at least one of the briefings and remembered that the Antonov was supposed to rock its wings to signal the moment to break formation and land. Most of the Minsk runway was behind us when James mimed a wing rock with his hands. 'Sapristi!' screamed the commander, obviously with visions of salt mines before him, as he ran the length of the cabin and flung himself into the cockpit, where he attempted to wrest the controls from the pilot in order to rock the wings.

Meanwhile, the formation had tightened up, and the Antonov pilot's knuckles were again glowing white on the control wheel. There ensued an altercation with the pilot trying hard to thrust the commander out of the cockpit without relinquishing his vice-like grip on the wheel.

According to James, their shouts practically drowned the engine noise. At about this time the navigator, a hulking mountain of a man, decided that in self-preservation something must be done, so he joined in what was by this time a full-blown brawl.

In complete contrast there was now nobody in charge of the aeroplane as it wallowed drunkenly about the sky, the cockpit full of flying fists. James was by this time thoroughly alarmed, understandably so, and was hanging on to his seat for dear life, there being no safety harness in the AN-2. I eased out wide, and noticed the other aircraft doing the same, as the antics in the cockpit of the 'Big Ant' could be plainly seen.

After what (at least to James) seemed an eternity, somebody got hold of the wheel, and the wings were mightily and majestically rocked, whereupon to the commander's indescribable relief we all landed in the appointed order.

Much to our surprise the engines ran well on the yellow-coloured fuel (strangely the Western counterpart, 80 octane, was red). Here at Minsk, and even at distant outposts like Vitebsk, where we night-stopped and where the fuel turned up in drums on a horse-drawn cart, the Russian refuellers were always meticulous. Each time they refuelled they produced a sample of fuel to be inspected for dirt or water; it was invariably clean, though never available at night. I never understood their reluctance to refuel as soon as we landed – perhaps they thought we might fly away in the night!

Finally we arrived at Toushino near Moscow, and rolled to a halt in the British parking bay. Determined, we leapt from the machines and instantly requested petrol. Heads were shaken. 'Tomorrow,' they said. We insisted on fuel and were told that the 80 octane bowser was locked in its compound for the night – only 100 was available. Very well, we would take 100 octane. They were incredulous. 'You can't run your engine on 100 octane!' they said. When we told them that it was merely to prevent condensation and that we would siphon it out in the morning, they were aghast. 'Anyway,' they said, 'there is no condensation in Russia!' Even as they spoke, a layer of mist was forming over the airfield! Then we had a brainwave! 'It is 'not permitted',' we said, 'to leave the aircraft overnight without fuel.' Now here was an argument they could understand. Within 2 minutes an 80 octane bowser pulled up in front of the Zlin. They even asked if we would like oil; 'Mazla' they called it, which is also their word for butter. We declined – the Zlin hadn't used any all the way from England.

Our fears about the quality of fuel proved groundless; all the engines ran perfectly, and with the contest under way a fuel truck appeared almost before the propeller stopped after each landing. The Zlin acquitted itself honourably, becoming the first 'British' aeroplane to reach the finals of any World Championship, so it was with a sense of achievement that we started on our long journey home. Again we were impressed by the minute attention to detail shown by the refuellers all the way across

Russia, and indeed Poland too. With a sense of relief we left behind us first Russia, then Poland, and soon Bornholm was seen as a smudge on the distant horizon. Now we could relax, as a giant mobile tanker, bristling with dials and levers, drew up in front of us as we shut down. Refuelling was fast and smooth, and we were quickly on our way again.

We flew low across the unbroken expanse of the Baltic, in loose formation, without even a ship in sight anywhere. Then the engine cut, 20 feet above the sea, the propeller windmilling! I prepared to jettison the canopy and jump, rather than risk ditching with a fixed undercarriage. Even as I reached for the jettison handle, the engine coughed, spluttered and picked up again! At full power, but sounding rough, I climbed the Zlin – altitude was safety. Now navigation was critical; I set course for Sonderborg, the nearest field, but in spite of the rough running and an occasional cough, the engine kept going, and with an enormous feeling of relief I felt her settle on to the runway.

I opened the cowlings and removed the fuel filters. In the bowl of the 'inverted' system filter was yellow petrol from Moscow – we had been in 'normal' flight ever since – and the fuel was clear and uncontaminated. Next I checked the 'normal' filter, full of red-coloured fuel from the shiny tanker in Bornholm, our first stop in the West – and in the bottom were great globules of water! I cleaned both filters, checked a sample from the airfield pump, which was clear, and reassembled the filters before refuelling. We had no more trouble. But who would have believed that we could fly twice across Russia using primitive refuelling facilities without trouble, then encounter such a heart-stopping situation caused by water contamination from a splendidly equipped modern Western refuelling station?

All that glitters is not gold, especially where aeroplanes are concerned.

18

... we regularly scraped over the hedge with heart in mouth and nothing to spare.' 'Great stuff!' the director would say. 'Do it again!'

'Aces High'

ONE hears so often of a feature flying film being planned, only to find that in the end it fails to materialise, that one learns not to become excited at the prospect of taking part. So when we heard that a flying film, entitled *Aces High* and based on the classic First World War play *Journey's End*, was being planned, we half expected it to go the way of the others. It wasn't until I walked into the hangar at Booker one day to find an electric atmosphere of activity, with three Stampes being feverishly transformed into SE5a replicas, that I really began to believe that this time it was going to come off. We were eventually to increase the film fleet to quite a mixed bag, for apart from the SE5as we were to finish up with a Viima, Tiger Moth, two Jungmeisters, and two replicas, of a Fokker Eindekker and a Morane Bullet. The startling paint schemes on some of these aeroplanes was sufficient to alter their otherwise unmodified outlines, and with Tony Bianchi wearing the chief pilot's hat, assisted by James Gilbert, Iain Weston and myself, we prepared to go to war. With Benny Fisz of *Battle of Britain* movie fame as producer, and Jack Gold directing, we were determined to give our best.

Originally we were only scheduled for a few days filming, but as time went on it became obvious that the film people were going to rely less on filming with model aircraft (as they had planned) and more and more on the real thing. Working in close harmony with the director of the aerial scenes, Derek Cracknell, we soon became mutually aware of each other's problems, with the result that the flying was not only very effective, but profoundly enjoyable. After three months of it we felt ready to take on the Red Baron himself!

We started off on the 'easy' shots, but very soon came up against a few basic problems. Working on the film set in the north-west corner of Booker airfield, where a replica of a First World War aerodrome had been built, we were surrounded by club aeroplanes and gliders. Not only that, but we were required always to take off towards the 'enemy lines', and land in the opposite direction, and since the afternoon sun could be made on film to look like dawn, not only were we never sure where 'east' or 'west' were supposed to be, but we invariably found that we had to take off and land downwind, or at best crosswind. Not only did this on occasion cause utter confusion in the Booker circuit, but in the small space available, and with the SE5as performing on take-off like the proverbial shot duck, we regularly scraped over the hedge with heart in mouth and nothing to spare. 'Great stuff!' the director would say. 'Do it again!' Some of the downwind formation take-offs were even more hairy, and it became noticeable that as the film progressed the SEs were becoming more and more tired, so that even when we took a longer run at it we finished by clearing the hedge by an even more insignificant margin. 'Great stuff!' said the director. 'Do it again!'

Becoming put off by these hedge-trimming operations quite early on, I volunteered to play the part of the wicked Hun; at least I wouldn't have to do any take-off shots! I should have known better, because the first combat shot of the film involved flying the Fokker Eindekker in a dogfight with an SE5a, historically unlikely and practically impossible. As in all flying films, the director was never fully convinced that a victory would be confirmed in the cinemagoer's eyes unless the victim burst into flames. This, however, not only prolongs the film, but is expensive in pilot and aircraft replacement, so one has to make do with smoke bombs. These contraptions were attached to the underside of the aeroplane, usually near carburettors, fuel filters and so on, and were electrically fired from the cockpit. One had to carry out a very careful pre-flight each day, as these appendages seemed to materialise overnight – the special effects department was extremely enthusiastic. Having insisted that these bombs were placed on the undercarriage struts, we proceeded with the shot. It was not a success. The Fokker suffered from wing flutter when dived to 70 knots, and the wings flexed in the most alarming manner during manoeuvres. To be on the safe side I reduced speed, whereupon the SE5a stalled and fell out of the sky. The fiasco by now well under way, I pressed the button to fire the smoke bombs and was promptly enveloped with thick acrid black smoke, which made my eyes stream and almost completely prevented breathing. We later found out that pilots in *The Blue Max* and other films had used breathing apparatus. I'm not surprised. Finally, and surprisingly quickly, the smoke stopped, to my great relief. I would have been less relieved had I known that the mounting brackets had melted and that the still-smoking bombs had disappeared earthwards! The Bianchi design department got to work and produced some very neat heatproof brackets, which operated very well, except that with the advent of the colder weather the toxic content of the smoke seemed to increase, and now not only did the 'victim' land looking as though he had been down a coal mine, he had a miner's cough to go with it!

Aerodynamically the SE5as were very good in one respect only – they did not asphyxiate the pilot, whereas the Viima and the Eindekker had little to choose between them in this respect. Indeed, one could clearly see the enshrouding envelope of smoke around the 'German' pilot after a successful attack. Perhaps the most spectacular sight in the air was when a forward-facing camera was in use and we closed to almost zero range behind our smoking victim as he twisted and turned low over the trees. Incandescent debris detached and hurtled backwards towards the camera; the first time I saw it I really thought he was on fire.

Most of the original dogfights took place at altitude, but every film director insists that one must engage in combat below tree-top height if it is to look realistic! For this exercise we obtained CAA clearance to operate out of a farmer's field liberally sprinkled with trees and copses. With the advantage of being away from the airfield, we were able for the first time to appreciate the incredible freedom of pure flying, with no regulations or restrictions. We also very quickly realised how, without a high degree of self-discipline, this could degenerate into a dangerous situation. Our first attempts to operate here with the Eindekker were so potentially dangerous that we quickly replaced it with the Viima, but even with the extra power, solidity and control it was still not a pleasant experience to dodge in and out of the trees fighting the slipstream of the SE5a ahead. We were appalled when we saw the rushes and realised that though we had been only 15 feet behind, the wide-angle lens had made the distance look like 20 yards. This would never do, but it would have been suicide to fly closer. The other problem was that with an aft-facing camera on the lead aircraft, the slightest sharp manoeuvre would swing the field of view away from the following machine – another reason why we had to fly much closer. We experimented, and found that we could fly directly in the leader's slipstream, so close that it actually stabilised the following aircraft. With only 4 feet between rudder and spinner, the slightest rudder pressure could cause enough asymmetric slipstream to roll on bank quickly to follow the manoeuvring aircraft ahead. We were almost being towed along by the 'victim', except that to stay close the leader had to fly at one-third throttle, while the attacker used full power to overcome the downwash – a most unnatural thing to do with a separation of only 4 feet!

We also found problems in the standard quarter attack. Normally one's guns are pointed ahead of the target, so that it intercepts the bullets at a predetermined point in space. With a camera one has to hold the target centrally in the frame, and with a fixed camera one inevitably finishes up flying a curve of pursuit to finish in line astern, which may not be what the director wants. To achieve the illusion of the quarter attack, the 'victim' has to fly as slowly as possible (the ideal would be to hover), while the attacker keeps his speed up. With a rather tired SE5a the speed differential was still only about 50mph, but even this was quite fast enough when one had a 35mm camera mounted directly in front of the windscreen! We were expected to hold the attack to a very close range, and we frantically peered round or under the camera to keep the rapidly expanding target in view. To get the victim's point of view, ie that of an SE5a approaching to a very close range on a quarter attack, we had to resort to a helicopter.

Aces High was unusual in that much of the aerial combat was actually shot from the film aircraft, as opposed to the standard helicopter shots, and as a result looks even more realistic. But for some shots a helicopter was the only possible camera-ship, and for this a Jet Ranger was hired. To get really accurate and close attacking shots it was necessary for the helicopter to fly as slowly as possible – hovering was out of the question because of the vibration and buffeting around the camera platform – but even at 30 knots the SE5as, at full power, were struggling to cross ahead of the chopper from an astern attack. The slow-flying helicopter often seemed to have an almost hypnotic quality in that it was difficult to appreciate the true closing speed until the last moment, and on one occasion, when the attacker seemed in some danger of getting behind the helicopter and going out of shot, the cameraman shouted to the chopper pilot to yaw, which he did, and promptly placed the helicopter directly in the path of the hard-turning SE5a. We began to learn something of the difficulties of this sort of operation, and to understand how easily an accident could occur. Although the intention was to have air-to-air radio communication, in practice these seldom worked, so each shot had to be thoroughly briefed on the ground; the aerobatic card-holders on the Stampe/SE5a instrument panels now contained the sortie brief, broken down into exercises, and identified by means of extended digits in the helicopter cabin. Close formation with the helicopter soon became the norm, in spite of our initial uneasiness at the proximity of the whirling rotor blades; eventually we learned the patterns of the rotor slipstream, and also, after several teeth-rattling jolts, we learned never to fly under a near-hovering helicopter.

As time went on it became obvious that there were several shots that we just could not get with normal camera positions – in particular shooting straight forward or back, and panning 360 degrees in azimuth. The problem was solved when a device named 'Astrovision', which had been previously used for filming jet airliners, was tried out in an Aztec. It consisted of a periscope protruding through the belly of the aeroplane, with a camera mounted inside the cabin. This assembly was remotely controlled from the rear seat by means of a pressure-sensitive control stick, which as well as full freedom in azimuth also allowed a degree of pitch. A monitor screen in the rear of the cabin, carefully aligned when the aircraft was on the ground, showed the field of view of the camera at all times.

... we learned never to fly under a near-hovering helicopter.

Now we could really show some dogfight scenes, since we could allow the 'victim' to use full power, while the Aztec, using half flap, formated only a few feet behind. This was fine in level flight, but as soon as the target started to manoeuvre, the Aztec at 80mph or less was in pre-stall buffet, which caused camera vibration. In the end this was accepted, as it gave the shot more realism, but from the long-suffering Aztec pilot's point of view, as he sat in the right-hand seat (an insurance requirement), while I flew the aeroplane from the left, it must have seemed that the whole sortie was flown with the stall warning horn on. One of the most surprising features of this tail-chasing situation was the incredible power of the biplane's wingtip vortices. Reversing the turn in the Aztec, trying to stay on the SE5a's tail, I needed full rudder, aileron, and a lot of differential throttle, with the horn permanently screeching its warning. The inevitable occurred on several occasions, when the Aztec stalled and flicked out of the formation. It needed quite a bit of practice to hold that cavorting SE5a squarely in the centre of the windscreen! But the Aztec had its advantages: on a winter's day at nearly 10,000 feet with the heater fully on I felt really sorry for the three accompanying SE pilots as we cruised for more than an hour looking for the right sort of cloud background.

On another occasion we found too much cloud, and I had to make a slow descent on instruments, with a biplane locked firmly onto each wingtip. Most of the film aircraft had minimal instrumentation with the result that (without deliberate intent) we ended up flying them by feel alone.

One of the other major problems occurred when we were perhaps at 3,000 feet, alone in the sky, in the Fokker Eindekker (maximum speed 60 knots), unable to manoeuvre, then a modern club aeroplane hove into view over the horizon. At first he was amazed at the sight of such a frail contraption, but as his eyes lit on the black crosses and machine gun, one could almost see the transformation from Cessna to Sopwith Camel! We had no way of knowing what his skills were; he might have been a 30-hour pilot with no formation experience and no real idea of closing speeds. We could not escape, and could only hope to avoid his clumsy passes; now we really had to fight a defensive battle in earnest.

For the first time we could appreciate the vulnerability of the First World War pilot, and our opponent here was not even armed. In the end he would tire of the sport and disappear, and we could glide earthwards to the safety of the trees, but still with many an anxious backward glance.

How must a German balloon observer have felt, high in his basket, the ugly sausage-shaped balloon undulating on the end of its cable above his head, when he heard the hum of Hispano engines, and could then pick them out against the evening sky, three small specks, gradually taking shape – SE5as? Screaming into his telephone he would urge the winch crew to wind him down. Beneath him activity was feverish, orders being shouted, men running, and all the while the aircraft drawing closer.

In the lead SE5a, with the red pennants flying from the struts, I raised my hand, James and Tony nodded and started to drop back into low-level battle formation. I held 600 feet, and waited until I crossed the road that runs from Lane End to Marlow, then I eased down into the dive. I studied the active runway carefully: no club aircraft taking off, good, I had a clear run. A backward glance showed the other two SEs in position as I switched on the strobe light attached to the muzzles of my mock-up machine guns. I kept a constant dive angle, not getting too low, otherwise the camera would have picked up the trees that border the airfield. Now I could see the camera crew, behind the observer's basket, which was suspended for this shot, from a crane. Still in my headlong dive, I saw the observer bale out – but he only fell 5 feet on to a pile of mattresses and cardboard boxes. Because of the wide-angle lens, I had to leave the pull-out as late as possible, but I was aware of the jib of the crane reaching out towards me – 'Now'! And I broke hard to the left, wings vertical. When we saw the rushes it was disappointing; our break was too far away, but we could not get closer. This is where we had to be firm and not let ourselves be talked into anything, but Derek knew that we stuck to our limits, and he planned an alternative shot.

Sometimes the most horrific shots were the easiest and safest. As the Viima pilot I was shot at the beginning of a take-off run, and the aircraft crashed out of control, into a copse, where it burst into flames. This shot took three days, and is completely realistic. First the actor pilot was wired up with explosive charges attached to capsules of imitation blood. A ground camera 'saw' a diving SE5a in the background; there was a rattle of machine-gun fire and the pilot, streaming with 'blood', collapsed. Now I changed places with the pilot, and climbed, rather squeamishly, into the synthetic blood-spattered cockpit. The cameraman, lashed onto a cradle on the wing, filmed the observer, panic-stricken, as the aircraft taxied across the field. Finally a ground camera filmed the aircraft, tail-up, heading straight for the wood; in plenty of time I cut the power and swung off to one side.

Next day, a camera was set up inside the copse. The aircraft, tail lashed on to a Land Rover, was positioned only feet from the edge of the copse, and the engine was started. The camera turned and the Land Rover drove away, towing the aircraft backwards. When the film is run in reverse it really looks like a collision! Finally an explosive charge was planted in the wood. As I took off, just to one side, all I heard was a muffled explosion. As I turned and looked back, a pall of black smoke hung over the copse, where a mock-up of the Viima burned steadily. Perfect!

As a result of their continuous use of explosives the special effects team tended to trigger everything by this means. For one shot a metal box was attached to the wing of the Eindekker adjacent to the pilot's right elbow. This box contained debris that (as a change from the usual smoke bomb) would signify a hit. It was, however, to be activated by an explosive charge. Now we pilots, and especially us Fokker pilots, had a very high concern for our skins, so it was decided to stage a ground demonstration, with the engine running. When a volunteer was called for to sit in the cockpit, the four pilots retreated to a safe distance, whereupon Doug Bianchi offered to ignite the device. The pilots retreated even further back and Doug, evidently suspecting that we might know something that he didn't, handed over control to a special effects man, who quite cheerfully pressed the button and vanished in a blinding flash and a cloud of dust. By this time the pilots (plus Doug) were further away from the Fokker than ever, having decided that the machine was bad enough to fly at the best of times, without an explosive box practically in the cockpit. We finally gave up flying the Fokker when Doug saw the wings flexing from the ground!

But perhaps the actors had the worst of it. I have never seen people so nearly blown up or set on fire on so many occasions. Indeed, we set one actual aircraft alight several times, fortunately on the ground and with fire services standing by. On one occasion Christopher Plummer was practically lifted out of his cockpit by one over-enthusiastic explosion! Perhaps the most frightening static shot was made by Roy Scammell, a totally fearless stuntman, who was clothed in Nomex, sprayed with petroleum jelly, then literally set on fire in the cockpit. He then leapt from the cockpit, on to the waiting mattresses, on fire from head to toe, to be then put out by CO_2 extinguishers. One could easily appreciate why so many First World War pilots chose to leap to their death rather than stay in the aircraft and burn.

Then, suddenly, it was all over; no more shivering round the tea urn at first light on a frost-covered airfield; no more cruising at 7,000 feet, using the

Viima as a camera ship while our expert cameraman, Peter Allwork, fought against the slipstream to steady the camera in sub-zero temperatures. There was barely time to say our goodbyes, but though the film was over, something remained. The pilots who had worked together for nearly four months had begun to realise the value of teamwork, and had come to place implicit trust in the others, something that is not too common these days in civil aviation, but is found more at squadron level in the armed forces. More than anything else, this film had brought home to us a tremendous admiration for those early pilots, too many of whom found that the road to France in 1917 was indeed for them Journey's End.

19

The Shvetstov was running steadily enough, although it sounded like an asthmatic farm tractor.

Russian Encounter

THE sight of a Russian Yak 11, complete with red stars, has caused many an airshow spectator to come and ask, 'Is it a real one?' And well they might ask this question, since there is only one operational Yak 11 in the western world.

The first time I came into contact with the aeroplane was when Doug Bianchi rang me up and asked if I would like to do the test flying. Vaguely suspecting a leg-pull, but not wishing to miss such an opportunity, I leapt at the chance. Any doubts were soon dispelled, for there, in the murky recesses of the hangar, in a rather dilapidated condition, stood the battered but recognisable components of a Yak 11 two-seat fighter trainer. Greatly interested, I poked about examining the details of the machine; even in that light it looked powerful and agile, with sharply pointed wings and a massive Shvetstov radial engine.

The aircraft had been acquired in a curious way. To begin with it had been built after the war, in 1956, in Czechoslovakia, and was one of a batch of twenty being delivered to Egypt. However, during the delivery flight it had suffered an engine malfunction over Cyprus, and had crash-landed on Morphou beach, on the north-west coast of the island. Having been 'written off', it found its way to Famagusta, where it was used to attract customers to a local garage; there it was found by an English businessman, who bought it and had it shipped back to England, and delivered to Booker for restoration by Personal Plane Services. The work was slow and difficult, with insufficient technical data, but one by one the problems were overcome, and gradually the aircraft was restored to its original condition. Perhaps the most difficult item was the engine, for the cause of the original failure had still not been found.

Now, on successive ground runs, the big radial bellowed its song of power, as if demanding to be allowed to fly again.

I spent some time sitting in the cockpit, familiarising myself with the controls and running the engine, for although I had flown the aerobatic Yak 18, it was a very different kettle of fish from this bulky monster.

At last the great day dawned, and as I walked out to the aeroplane I saw that the compressed-air bottle was already connected, for the Yak is entirely dependent on air for all its systems, including engine starting. Quickly I strapped in, while the mechanics fussed over last-minute details, polishing the windscreen and canopy, and generally exhibiting the usual symptoms of nervousness associated with any first flight. Finally I was ready: fuel cock on, and I pumped up some pressure before injecting neat fuel into the manifold, using the yellow-painted hand primer. All systems are colour-coded, yellow for petrol, brown for oil, etc. As this was going on the aircraft air bottles were being charged from the ground equipment air bottle. Maintaining ground bottle pressure, I switched on the magnetos, opened the ICO, pressed the booster coil button and opened the starter air valve.

One felt rather short of hands at this juncture, as the stick had to be held back and the throttle pumped as the 820hp Shvetstov radial started to

turn. The engine emitted the odd puff of smoke and spasmodic cough before suddenly catching with a deep roar and a cloud of blue smoke. It was important to remember to screw the air starter valve closed, because the conservation of air pressure was of vital importance. I elected to run up the engine on the chocks, because there was no parking brake, and the use of brakes depleted the air pressure in the most alarming fashion. I later discovered that one had to conserve air pressure carefully while taxiing, otherwise one could find oneself airborne with insufficient pressure to retract the undercarriage! I throttled back, waved the chocks away, and taxied slowly out to the threshold, swinging the great round nose from side to side.

The close-cropped grass, edged by white marker boards, stretched away into the distance, the far hedge invisible over the gentle rise that marked the middle of the airfield. I aligned the aircraft carefully, and pulled the stick fully back to lock the tailwheel central. Brakes on, I slowly opened the throttle. The rumble of the Shvetstov increased to a deep growl as the throttle reached the rated power stop; then I pulled the trigger and moved the throttle lever wide open. The growl swelled to a roar, and the aircraft bucked and kicked against the brakes. With a hiss of escaping air, I released the brake lever, and the Yak lumbered ponderously forward, disappointingly slowly at first. As rudder control became available, I pushed the stick forward, gently at first, then harder, for the speed was building up and the tail was still firmly on the ground. The sight of the markers flashing past the wingtips at least confirmed that I was still in the middle of the runway, for I could see nothing in front of me except that great engine.

As I was on the point of abandoning take-off, the tail rose sluggishly, presenting me with my first sight of the airfield over the nose. It also brought home another fact: airspeed 80 knots, over half the airfield already used, and no idea of stalling speed! None of the books that had come with the aircraft had mentioned stalling speed and behaviour, and I was very conscious of the possibility of a tip stall and perhaps a wing drop.

The rate of acceleration seemed even lower as the far hedge loomed into view, but at 100 knots it seemed reasonable that the aircraft should fly, so I started to ease back on the stick very gently. Still she hammered along the ground, showing not the slightest inclination to fly; 105 knots on the clock, about 200 yards to go – something had to be done, and quickly! The flaps have only two positions, and the down position is used normally only for landing. They are pneumatically operated, and total travel takes less than a second. I flicked the lever back, there was a hiss of compressed air, a sudden trim shift, and the aircraft literally leapt into the air, clearing the hedge by a good 20 feet. I quickly selected gear up, but the aircraft was not apparently accelerating, so I was content to hold level flight at about 50 feet initially. Later I was to discover that although the aircraft was reluctant to accelerate above 100 knots with gear and flaps down, it would nevertheless demonstrate a respectable rate of climb at 95 knots.

With wheels and flaps retracted, I settled into the climb at 130 knots, throttling the much-maligned engine back through the gate to climbing boost. The Shvetstov was running steadily enough, although it sounded like an asthmatic farm tractor. In time one gets used to this! I levelled out at 5,000 feet and slowly, cautiously, started to explore the behaviour and performance of this strange machine. In the cruise it was stable and solid, although the noise level in the cockpit was very high. One gained the impression that the aircraft would make a very stable gun platform, but it was nowhere near as manoeuvrable as a Spitfire, though the rate of roll was very much higher, due to the fact that most of the weight is concentrated in the fuselage, the wings being very small and light. Acceleration was relatively slow, and the aircraft relied for its performance on the conversion from potential to kinetic energy and back again; now it was easy to see why the aerobatic Yak 18s, with the same balance of thrust and weight, played the yo-yo, relying almost entirely on vertical manoeuvres. The Yak 11, on a bigger scale, demanded to be flown in much the same manner, and aerobatics were a real joy.

In the dive, the controls became iron hard, but the Yak was stable and solid; like a giant express train, it seemed to be running on rails. The deep note of the engine was drowned in the banshee scream of air around the canopy as the needle of the ASI quivered on the VNE mark – 320 knots. I braced myself about the 'g' as I pressed back on the stick and the Yak, with its gigantic momentum, soared upwards in a clean vertical climb of more than 3,000 feet. But sitting just behind an 820hp engine has its disadvantages: the cockpit was intolerably hot; perhaps a good thing in a Siberian winter, but I found it necessary to open the forward-facing ram air vent, which admitted such a blast of air that goggles or sunglasses became a necessity. One could not keep one's unprotected eyes open in the face of this blast, yet one could not survive the baking heat without it.

Turning reluctantly from aerobatics to more mundane things, I found, as I had expected, that at the stall the aircraft was a wing-dropper, although if one was quick this could be kept down to 20°. What did surprise me was that the use of flap only lowered the stalling speed from 82 to 78 knots. When it stalled in a turn, it behaved very much like a Harvard, in that it flicked quite suddenly, to the right. Indeed, in a right-hand turn it was quicker to keep the roll going and complete the full 360 degrees than to try and stop it.

Armed with this information I set course towards the airfield, to see what other surprises were in store.

Back in the circuit I found that 130 knots downwind was quite fast enough, reducing to 100 knots when flaps and undercarriage were down. A long drag-in approach proved inadvisable, as the already poor view became negligible. It is surprising how much airfield can be hidden behind an engine! Even if the runway was short, I preferred to make a fairly steep curved approach, straightening out as late as possible.

At first I placed the aircraft rather hurriedly on its mainwheels (just above the ground is no place for a 20-degree wing drop), but I later found that the aircraft could be three-pointed power off. The extra aerodynamic drag associated with a stalled landing made the whole thing a much more gentlemanly affair, the aircraft sinking onto all three wheels with no tendency to bounce or drop a wing, and stopping comfortably on a runway 750 metres long, with no wind. With the stick held fully back, and the tailwheel locked fore and aft, a straight landing run was easy to maintain. The flapless landing needed exactly the same technique, ie a relatively slow, fairly steep approach, crossing the hedge at 95 to 90 knots, some 5 knots faster than with full flap. The aircraft much prefers to operate from a tarmac runway, as the undercarriage gives a hard ride on a grass surface, producing a sympathetic frequency at about 10mph, when the aircraft starts a mild bouncing, which very quickly magnifies into a series of kangaroo-like leaps. (Perhaps in Russia Yak pilots are first checked out on the four-legged variety!)

It is an interesting aircraft of the old school, and if one can cope with agile behaviour, especially at the stall, there is a good deal of satisfaction to be found in flying it. It is highly reminiscent of the very manoeuvrable Yak 18 of the Soviet Aerobatic Team, having the same ratio of pitching and rolling inertia, the same high rate of roll with light control forces, and the same incredibly low control circuit friction. Small wonder, then, that its aerobatic performance is quite startling, as anyone who has seen it perform at air displays will testify. In spite of the fact that there are no spare parts, it remains remarkably serviceable, demanding little in the way of attention.

The magnitude of the whole restoration task can be summed up by Doug's story of his attempts to gather information about the aircraft at the Paris Air Show, when he tried to chat up one of the Yakovlev team. All he could elicit was, 'You have not got a Yak!' Seeing, they say, is believing!

20

*'You're on fire!' I shouted, realising in the same
instant that he could not hear me.*

A Tiger to the Rescue

T HE display had been a good one and the locals were more than
friendly. Aeroplanes and pilots had been refuelled, and with some
reluctance we prepared to leave for our long flight south. We needed
two days for this, as we were at Castletown Aerodrome in Caithness, almost
as far north as you can go on the mainland of Britain.

One aircraft had already left on the previous day, the two-seat Tiger with
the standing-on-the-wing rig attached to the centre section. The drag was so
high that he could only cruise at 65 knots and needed the extra day's start.

Another pilot was looking sorrowfully at a broken propeller and
wondering whether to saw off any more blade, or to balance it by adding
woodscrews to the other end in an attempt to stop the engine from shaking
itself out of the airframe, while the Stampe refused point-blank to start at all.
The rest of us decided to go in pairs, as the terrain was generally
uninhabited, and it would not have been prudent to go alone.

We took off, gave the locals a farewell low run, and set course across some of the most barren country in Scotland. Peat bogs, marsh and heather were the order of the day; for mile after mile nothing moved on the ground, no vehicle (no roads), no trains (no railways) – not even a sheep. The sheer desolation was indescribable, and instinctively Jim and I closed up into tight formation. I was flying one of the single-seat racing Tigers, and it was going beautifully; I felt that Jim was a braver man than me in flying a Turbulent over such country (incidentally, the chairman's own machine, loaned to Jim for the trip).

These thoughts were interrupted by the realisation that Jim had dropped back a few yards, but was still flying steadily on course. As I watched, he slowed even more, until eventually he was several hundred yards behind. Feeling slightly irritated that he should break formation over such poor terrain, I rolled into a 360-degree turn to let him catch up. He flew straight past without even a glance at me as I levelled out alongside.

You're on fire!' I shouted

Irritation was mounting when suddenly I realised he was in trouble. The next second my heart nearly stopped altogether, as a great trail of white smoke erupted from his machine. 'You're on fire!' I shouted, realising in the same instant that he could not hear me.

The ground was completely unsuitable for any sort of landing, but the map showed that the coast was only a few miles ahead. Jim was obviously trying to reach this area, but could he make it? The smoke became thicker and trailed 40 feet behind the aeroplane, when we suddenly crossed a low hill and there, below us, was a clear, calm loch. But more important, alongside the loch was a beautiful field, big enough to land a Turbulent.

Jim shut the throttle and spiralled left, while I followed him down, carefully keeping out of his way.

The picture is still imprinted on my mind: the loch, the hills covered with heather, a tiny dark blue aeroplane with a white smoke trail and a beautiful green field. Jim straightened low over the water, his reflection almost touching him, the smoke still persistent. As I got lower, I saw that the field was very rough, apart from a narrow strip in the centre.

Suddenly I realised that what I thought was smoke was in fact oil.

The Turbulent's windscreen was black with oil and I feared that the landing was rapidly becoming impossible. But with falling oil pressure there is no choice, and with relief and admiration I saw the tailskid bite into the turf just inside the field. What a sight I saw as I overshot – cowlings, wings and windscreen were glistening black with oil, but Jim sat there unconcerned and waved.

Now it was my turn! I brought the Tiger in as slowly as I dared, low over the water, and as the grass appeared behind my wing, cut the throttle. The Tiger bounced, touched down again and lurched to a halt. The silence could almost be felt when I switched off, for there was no sign of life apart from a few sheep who stared at us dully.

We took off the Turbulent's cowlings, cleaned off the oil, and started up. Immediately a jet of black oil squirted into the air, and we quickly switched off. We found that we needed a new oil pipe; it was fractured, and impossible to repair.

Darkness was a couple of hours away, but I didn't want to leave Jim alone in that wilderness. Looking at the map, we found that we were exactly on track; the other pilots en route to Inverness should have spotted us, but we had to console ourselves with pointed remarks about their navigation.

We saw nothing, and we needed a two-seat aeroplane to get Jim back to civilisation. As I cursed the fact that I was flying a single-seat Tiger, a crazy thought struck me.

This was a special Tiger, stripped, light, and with a powerful engine – powerful enough to lift both of us (one out in the slipstream) over the hills that surrounded the loch? It was worth a try.

We picketed and covered the Turbulent and removed the luggage that occupied the space normally taken by a standard Tiger's front cockpit. Jim found that by standing on the pickets and holding on to the centre-section struts, his head was level with the top wing. He was game to try it.

... with a final bounce we were airborne!

We paced out the field and found that the level strip was 50 yards, with a good over-run. We started the engine, and Jim climbed aboard. He packed himself in with all the baggage and, last of all, took on board the wooden cockpit cover, which he wedged in over his knees as a sort of windscreen.

Jim pronounced all systems 'go', and I prepared for take-off. Even the sheep were taking an interest by this time.

We taxied downwind towards the loch and turned into wind. The idiot sheep stared blankly as Jim pulled down his goggles and nodded. The wind was about 15 knots as I opened the throttle. The tail rose slowly and the flock of sheep got nearer. At 25 knots I started pulling and with a final bounce we were airborne! The sheep did very creditable bomb bursts beneath us as we slowly gathered climbing speed. Jim hung on grimly, with beard and moustaches fluttering, and his flying jacket billowing out behind him. One could be led to believe that his ancestors had sailed in long ships – he looked the picture of a Viking, thirsting for the spoils of war!

Meanwhile the Tiger circled, climbing slowly. What an aeroplane! But now I was becoming concerned, because I was using full throttle, and the slipstream and cold would be weakening Jim.

But at last we cleared the hills and I could throttle back slightly. Every now and then Jim half turned and nodded, signifying that he was OK, and soon Inverness appeared before us.

The Tiger handled almost normally, in spite of its unusual burden, and as we taxied clear of the runway, Jim was grinning; he seemed to have quite enjoyed the experience!

Not so the display co-ordinator, who had almost given us up. The expression on his face when he saw our Tiger apparently festooned with humanity, and simultaneously realised that the chairman's personal aeroplane must have come to grief, made the whole escapade seem worthwhile.

A seat was found for Jim in one of the touring aeroplanes, and late the next day we taxied up to the clubhouse, home at last. There was a great deal of laughter and leg-pulling when the story got about, but in the end it was the chairman who had the last word, when he heard what had happened to his aeroplane. 'Go back and get it,' he said!

21

...at full power she was consuming more than 260 gallons per hour, and even at reduced power in aerobatics the consumption was 180-200gph.

Sea Fury

WITH eighteen cylinders producing 2,480hp, the Sea Fury is just about the fastest piston-engined fighter ever. The handling is surprisingly docile for such a high-performance machine. But the fuel consumption is 60gph at cruise, 260gph at full throttle!

When the Typhoon entered service in the autumn of 1941 it was soon found that there were compressibility problems (which included aileron reversal) at speeds of more than 500mph caused mainly by the very thick wing section. It was thought that by reducing this from 18% to 14% the aircraft would be stable at very much higher speeds. The result was the Hawker Tempest, but such is the rate of progress in wartime that soon after the first flight of the prototype Tempest, Hawker was already thinking about a new fighter, smaller and lighter, with a bigger engine, known as the Tempest Light Fighter (Centaurus). This project soon merged with a new requirement for a naval fighter, and resulted in the Hawker Fury for both the RAF and the Royal Navy. Various power plants were installed in the new aircraft, including a Rolls-Royce Griffon with contra-rotating propellers; the Bristol Centaurus sleeve-valve radial; and one prototype was fitted with a Napier Sabre, which made it the fastest of all Hawker piston-engined fighters. There had been vibration difficulties in the early days with the four-bladed Rotol propeller fitted to the Centaurus, and this had been cured by using a five-bladed propeller.

Towards the end of the war the Fury contract for the RAF was cancelled, and the new aircraft, now known as the Sea Fury, became essentially a post-war aeroplane. In the next seven years more than 600 Sea Furies were delivered to the Royal Navy, and the type became the Fleet Air Arm's principal single-seat fighter until replaced by jets in 1953. Although it was not operational in the European theatre during the Second World War, the Sea Fury saw combat in Korea, and was responsible for destroying a number of MiG15s.

The two-seat Fury trainer was initially produced for the Iraqi Air Force, and was later accepted by the Royal Navy, though it did not go to sea; perhaps the view from the rear cockpit precluded dual deck landings! Initially the canopies were two single bubbles, but after one of the rear canopies collapsed during trials the interconnecting cockpit canopy was added.

In 1957 a number of two-seat Sea Furies were refurbished by Hawker, and ten TT Mk 20 aircraft were sold to Deutsche Luftfahrt Beratungsdienst for target-towing duties, and were modified in Germany with a Swiss-designed winch. In recent years a number of these aircraft were acquired by Doug Arnold, who had them ferried back to Blackbushe, to be sold to private individuals. Now it is one thing to go out and buy a Sea Fury, but the next problem that arises is how to move it to one's home airfield? And when the chairman of the Elstree Flying Club, Spencer Flack, became the proud owner of Hawker Sea Fury G-BCOW he wisely decided that he wanted more than the available 2,500 feet at Elstree to embark on his first solo, at which point I became involved in the exercise. Apparently nobody thought to ask me how I felt about landing at Elstree on my first solo on type, so I decided to carry out some full-stop landings at Blackbushe to see how much room I needed. We chose Boxing Day to ferry the aircraft across, mainly because the weather was fair, and especially because there was a 10-knot wind blowing straight down Runway 27 at Elstree. As it happened, both airfields were practically deserted, so I was not to be embarrassed by having to avoid the local club aircraft. With no radio I had arranged to wing-rock and divert if I didn't like the approach to Elstree.

We travelled down to Blackbushe in style in the chairman's King Air, and I took the opportunity of noting ground features that were equal to the destination runway length as we circled prior to landing. For a single-engined machine the Sea Fury is quite a big aeroplane, and this feeling is accentuated as one approaches it – it towers over the pilot, and indeed there are three footholds provided for the climb into the cockpit. With any of the big piston-engined fighters one has to think of the size of the engine and propeller compared with the size of the fin and rudder, and for maximum effect in the case of the Sea Fury this comparison ought to be made when standing on the wing. When one looks at the great engine cowling housing an eighteen-cylinder engine of 2,480hp, surmounted by a five-bladed propeller of about 14 feet diameter, the fin and rudder look very insignificant. I consoled myself with the thought of the wide-track undercarriage as I clambered aboard and settled into the seat, discovering that the cockpit is very small and tight, with elbow room at a distinct premium. This seemed quite surprising considering the bulk of the aeroplane. The throttle lever is particularly large, and in fact can be an obstruction in the case of an emergency evacuation; but I was to find that (especially on the approach) it resulted in very smooth and precise engine control due to its low gearing. Once settled in, the amount of room in the cockpit was not unreasonable, except that one could not easily reach or see controls or instruments on the rear of the side panels.

Having done my homework with the Pilot's Notes the day before, things were reasonably familiar as I checked the cockpit, and I followed the priming drill religiously, giving the injector a full 30 seconds priming and the cylinders 10 seconds on the separate push-buttons. Brakes on, throttle set and mags on, and I pushed and held the starter button, simultaneously firing the cartridge in the Coffman starter and energising the booster coil. The propeller turned surprisingly slowly as I blipped the cylinder primer button, the gigantic blades marching past the windscreen like a column of guardsmen. I flicked the ICO to run and advanced the throttle, and watched the rev counter climbing slowly as the Centaurus lit up. There was very little to check as the engine warmed up; I exercised the flaps, noting that the lever was a little too

close to the undercarriage lever for my liking. As the temperatures and pressures rose I opened up to zero boost, the harsh bark of the exhaust swelling to a deep roar, while one could feel the slap of the propeller blade wash against the cockpit. I checked the magnetos and propeller and exercised the supercharger, all the while ready to cut the power instantly should the tail start to rise, but there was no problem. Although she had not flown for more than a year, the engine sounded clean and powerful. I throttled back and waved the chocks away. With the tailwheel unlocked she steered easily on the brakes; although they are pneumatically operated via a brake lever on the stick and a dual relay valve on the rudder bar, like a Spitfire, the wide track undercarriage gives much better directional control, and although the mass of the aeroplane is greater, there is less of a tendency to swing.

I lined up on the runway and locked the tailwheel; it is locked fore and aft and cannot be steered. I had elected to use take-off flap because I wanted to familiarise myself with the unassisted carrier technique, which I would need on subsequent take-offs at Elstree. The normal airfield take-off does not require the use of flaps. The book also suggests that the hood be left open for take-off and landing, but experience with Spitfires has proved that one thinks more clearly without the devastating racket of a big piston engine thundering about one's unprotected head. I cranked the hood closed and locked it. I wound the rudder trim fully left, pausing momentarily to remind myself that this machine would try to swing in the opposite direction to a Merlin-powered aeroplane, and finally I twisted in the cockpit to ensure that the wing fold lever was in the spread and locked position, and checked that the red indicator buttons on the wings were flush. Unlike the Spitfire, the book recommends the use of full power for take-off – try that with a Spitfire and the aeroplane will swap ends with great rapidity!

As in most big single-seaters of that period, the view forward from the Fury cockpit was nil so, keeping straight by referring to the edge of the runway, I released the brakes and steadily opened the throttle. The engine response was very smooth indeed, and sitting so high above the ground I was not really aware of a high rate of acceleration. It is only by referring to the ASI and the distance consumed along the runway that one becomes aware that this beast is not hanging about! As the boost reached +6lb the tail came off the ground, and I deliberately held it a little low, remembering the enormous diameter of the propeller. The deep roar of the engine seemed muffled compared to the snarl of a Merlin, and I was only aware of the long relentless surge forward. I pushed the throttle wide open to give +9½lb boost, and only now did I feel her trying to crab to the right – no wonder the tread wears quickly on the right tyre! Holding her straight with hard left rudder, I eased on a little left aileron to counteract the drift, then she lifted gently and cleanly, still trying to drift to the right, but nicely in trim and accelerating fast.

I flicked the brakes on and off, stretching forward to release the catch on the undercarriage lever before selecting up. Leaving full throttle set, I pulled the rpm lever fully back into the auto position; the revs flickered and settled at 2,650rpm. Now I could forget about pitch and just use the throttle in the rpm interconnect mode. By now the gear was up and the IAS was rising through 150 knots, so I selected flaps up; although the book mentioned a nose-up trim change, this was much less than I expected. The Centaurus is an extremely flexible and smooth engine, and it gave not a moment's trouble. As I retrimmed the rudder, and eased the power back to +4lb, it dawned on me that this aeroplane was not the vicious brute I had half expected, but a big solid gentle machine. It has many of the characteristics of the Spitfire in that it is directionally sensitive to changes of power and speed, and the trim curve in the medium-speed band is quite flat, but its response is more subdued than a Spitfire, and it needs less attention from the pilot in normal flying. The ailerons, however, are excellent, with their torque-tube-operated spring tabs; they feel well balanced and precise. In many ways the aeroplane handles rather like a jet, apart from the directional trim problems, especially in that it came as rather a surprise to look at the ASI and realise just what speed it was doing.

But there was work to be done; I had to find out how best to land this machine. Unlike most aircraft of this size, there is no real cooling problem in normal handling, so it was not necessary to open the engine cooling shutters for a stall approach; indeed, when the shutters are open it increases the stalling speed by 5 knots as well as causing additional buffet. I advanced the rpm lever to give 2,400rpm (approach revs) and closed the throttle. A red light glared at me from the instrument panel to tell me that the undercarriage was still up. As I reduced speed, there was the occasional snatch felt through the aileron circuit, with a lightening of stick force, and the nose and left wing dropped gently at 95 knots. So much for the clean stall – now for the interesting bit. I lowered wheels and flaps and again reduced speed, expecting, after the usual aileron snatching, to encounter a right wing drop (according to the Pilot's Notes). This could be a problem on an approach, because the sudden application of full power could cause a torque roll to the right and could result in a stall/spin accident.

With several thousand feet of air beneath me, I awaited events, and after the occasional twitch on the ailerons the left wing dropped, as before. I checked forward and eased on climb power, keeping the top needle central, and instantly she recovered and started to climb away. I repeated the exercise with and without power, but there was no sign of a torque stall, though it was always the left wing that dropped. Perhaps if the right wing had gone down it would have been a different story. At this point I felt that I had earned some relaxation, so with the aircraft clean again I opened up the power to +6 and eased the nose down. The speed rose extremely quickly, and from 320 knots a loop was a relatively prolonged exercise, consuming almost 4,000 feet, but the main points were the rate at which the speed built up during the exit from the manoeuvre, and the potential height loss involved if one was not careful. Barrel rolls were effortless, such was the power and response of the ailerons, but another disadvantage of the Sea Fury was evident: at full power she was consuming more than 260 gallons per hour, and even at reduced power in aerobatics the consumption was 180-200gph, and I had only started with fuselage fuel – about 120 gallons. With the propeller in auto and the throttle closed, she was very slow to lose speed, and I had to set 2,400rpm to use the propeller as an airbrake; as it was, I went around the Blackbushe circuit twice before she slowed down and descended to 1,000 feet.

I selected wheels down and flaps to max lift, but left the tailwheel locked, this being the only difference between an airfield landing and a carrier landing. Obviously the hook engaging in the arrester wire takes the swing out of a landing and leaves the aircraft manoeuvrable on the deck. The carrier approach is made at stalling speed plus 10 knots, so I rounded the figure up to 90 knots. I flew a steady curved final, lowering full flap as I straightened and settling down at 90 knots on a shallow approach. I had still not found it necessary to touch the elevator trim, and as on take-off I kept the hood shut. I had selected a point on the runway equivalent to the available distance at Elstree, but now I was concentrating entirely on the threshold. The slightest reduction of speed caused the nose to rise in an exaggerated manner in an instinctive attempt to hold the glide-path, and coincident with this was a determined yaw to the right, which felt distinctly uncomfortable. As I got more accustomed to the fine engine adjustment due to the long throttle lever, I was able to hold a steady attitude and fly the glide-path using power alone.

Remembering what the book had said about needing to get the stick well back to three-point, as I crossed the hedge I simultaneously closed the throttle and hauled back on the stick. Instantly the tail came down, and with no appreciable float she was on the ground and running straight. I braked quite hard, and she stopped in what seemed a ridiculously short distance. I could scarcely believe it: a landing run only 100 yards longer than the King Air! Gradually it dawned on me that it had shown not the slightest tendency to swing, and I began to realise the wide gulf in handling ease that separated this machine from the earlier fighters of the last war. I retracted the flaps to the take-off position, wound the rudder trim fully left, opened the engine cooling shutters, and with most of the main runway still in front of me I decided to take off again immediately: I wanted to get airborne to cool the brakes.

Again the take-off was straightforward, with very little tendency to swing – just that strong drift to the right as the last few pounds of boost came on. This time I throttled back and turned downwind, still flying a relatively big circuit to give myself time to settle down on finals. Again I noted the difference between this and a Spitfire when I was on finals; in a Spitfire I would not have been able to see the airfield, let alone the runway, but the sloping nose of the Fury made the approach very easy – I could see everything. Again I cut the power and pulled the stick back, and she sat down with no fuss at all, and again stopped very quickly. I looked at the fuel state – 75 gallons, enough to have a go at Elstree and to divert. I ran through the checks, and this time I was ready for the tendency to go sideways at high power, and she lifted into the air with no more fuss than if she had been a Chipmunk. At +2lb boost she cruised at 250 knots with a consumption of only 60gph, arriving over Elstree just behind the King Air, which had had nearly 10 minutes' start.

There were a couple of club aircraft pottering around the circuit, which promptly scattered and vanished when 5 tons of Sea Fury slid menacingly into view. Turning at 250 knots is a protracted neck-creaking business, but the Fury maintained its docile behaviour, requiring very little input from the pilot. Unlike the Spitfire she showed no tendency to tighten the turn, the only real problem being the reluctance to slow down. I set up the approach just as I had practised and, with the notoriously poor undershoot area of Elstree ahead of me, I was again glad of the excellent view forward. Things were rapidly becoming easier with practice, and as I cut the power she settled nicely on three points, and stopped in about two-thirds of the runway without any real effort.

In the confined space at Elstree she looked enormous, and I had to fold the wings to taxi between the rows of parked aircraft, the bark of the Centaurus echoing painfully between the upright mainplanes. The most

dangerous part of the whole exercise was getting in and out of the aeroplane, but her appearance is certainly deceptive; she really is a sheep in wolf's clothing, especially when compared with other thirty-year-old military machines. One would ideally need a Service background to fly such an aeroplane to the limits required in an air display, but for normal flying from a 1,500-yard runway there is no reason why a competent PPL could not cope, with proper supervision and briefing. A short runway brings its own problems, requiring extremely accurate flying on the approach, with the added hazard of a torque stall if the pilot gets it wrong. Perhaps the only thing for the non-Service pilot to avoid is low-level aerobatic flying; the amount of height a Sea Fury consumes has to be seen to be believed, and all in the space of a very short time. But treated with the proper amount of respect, it is a very pleasant and rewarding aeroplane – if you can afford the fuel bill!

22

At the appointed time the Scimitar arrived, in a cloud of condensation, at nought feet. The squadron commander really excelled himself - it was as near Mach 1 as made no difference.

Mach Effects

OWADAYS, when it is thought commonplace for businessmen to fly across the Atlantic in excess of Mach 2, sipping their cocktails in comfort, it is perhaps worth casting one's thoughts back a few short years when supersonic flight was still in the future, and most military pilots were living in the era of transonic flight.

At about this time I was attached to a well-known unit in the South of England, as a trainee test pilot, after which I transferred to another flight that was involved with low-level weapons development. Before this I had never flown a fighter aircraft, having been brought up on trainers and bombers, so I looked forward eagerly to achieving the ambition of many a frustrated bomber pilot – flying a fighter aircraft faster than sound.

As with many things, however, this turned out to be something of an anti-climax, because in the first place there was no sensation associated with going supersonic, and second, I was so infernally busy trying to record an impossible number of parameters on my test cards, as well as fly the aeroplane, that I probably wouldn't have noticed any sensation anyway.

It seems old hat now, but at that time the Hunter Mk. 4, without drop tanks, was quite a lively aeroplane, especially to an ex-bomber pilot, so it was with a feeling of some importance that I announced to the world in general, and incidentally to the radar controller, that I was at 42,000 feet and ready for a 'boom flight'. I would then apply full power, roll into the dive, and with the stick held hard forward, try and get some idea of what was going on around me, and write it down legibly.

It seemed that it was only a few brief moments later that I would throttle back and extend the airbrakes at 10,000 feet, thoroughly confused, and with the test card covered with indecipherable hieroglyphics. Gradually the situation became less foreign to me and I was more aware of things happening, eventually discovering, among other things, that the best way to recover with the minimum loss of height was to leave full power on, airbrakes in, and simply pull back on the stick. Also the subsequent climb, the initial part of which was still supersonic, was quite awe-inspiring!

I managed to finish the programme inside the allotted time schedule, and found myself with one flight left with nothing more to explore, so I thought this would be a good opportunity to concentrate entirely on how fast I could get the Hunter to go.

At 42,000 feet I levelled out and accelerated at full throttle. As I approached the coast, flat out, I called 'ready to dive'. The controller cleared me to go, on a south-easterly heading, and I rolled to the inverted, still at full power, and eased the nose down until I was vertical, half rolling as I went through Mach 1 to point the right way in the recovery. I had passed a layer of cloud, only 500 feet thick, at 13,000 feet on the climb, and had decided to use this as a marker to start the pull-out.

The Hunter accelerated, the cloud rushing upwards towards me as the needle wound up through Mach 1 and beyond 1.05, the highest speed reached on the tests so far and still accelerating slowly, the speed only apparent from the rapidly expanding cloudscape. The clouds leapt at me with incredible velocity, and I started the pull-out. Fleeting instants of hurtling grey, and I was in the clear below cloud, the sea ahead of me empty – except for an ocean passenger liner!

There was no way the controller or I could have known it was there, and as the gunsight swept upwards across the ship's bridge I saw the Machmeter at its maximum reading – Mach 1.09. Seconds later I flashed back up through the cloud, in a near vertical climb. I have often wondered since at the consternation that I had caused on board the vessel; I had been well and truly supersonic from 38,000 feet downwards – the sonic bang must have destroyed all the glassware in the ship. I flew back sedately, expecting the worst, but after a few days, when nothing happened, I started to relax. After all, I supposed, worse things happen at sea!

Not long after this I was to see the effect of high-speed flight at high Mach numbers, especially at low level, when the cloudbase seems to accentuate the aural effects of transonic flight. By now we were operating with Scimitar aircraft, which although deficient in performance by modern standards, especially above 30,000 feet, were quite impressive, by our standards, at low level.

One of our exercises was to fly at a very low altitude, as fast as possible, along a marked strip across the airfield, which of course necessitated a long run in to settle down. It was the guaranteed cure for low-flying addicts, to have to do it with precision, day in and day out, but whether we were fed up or not, with practice we got quite good at it.

Because the locals got upset, quite understandably, by the colossal racket we made, we had to warn every farmhouse adjacent to the run-in line when we were carrying out these trials. It wasn't just the volume of noise they objected to, it was the shock factor of the cannon-like effect of a near sonic pass at low altitude.

One fine morning the squadron commander set off to fly just such a sortie, and the duty Land Rover went off its rounds of the farmhouses. Now this Land Rover was a rather aged vehicle and therefore incapable of anything more than a modest turn of speed, which, combined with our squadron commander, who was dead keen and very quick off the mark, resulted in the first pass being made before the Land Rover had finished its rounds.

It was a warm and peaceful morning, and the son and heir to the farm in question was fast asleep in his pram and, unlike our airborne hero, not strapped in. After all, a six-month-old baby cannot sit up unaided, much less bail out of his pram. With a shattering crack and a gargantuan roar

our squadron commander hurtled past, not 100 feet away, at which point
the farmer's pride and joy cleared his pram in a standing leap and finished
up on the grass alongside, where he proceeded to expand his tiny lungs and
compete for noise honours with the Scimitar. It was a long time before we
heard the end of that one! Compliments on the baby's reaction time were
not favourably received.

Our squadron commander had another brush with the locals at
about this time, after a lady had complained that low-flying aircraft had
shattered her chandelier. When this happened a second time (to the same
lady) we thought we would investigate further. Our ancient Land Rover
was VHF-equipped, so it was positioned in a lane, not very far from the
rather stately country house in question. After all, there was a limit to the

Compliments on the baby's reaction time were not favourably received.

number of chandeliers the Air Force could be expected to replace. At the appointed time the Scimitar arrived, in a cloud of condensation, at nought feet. The squadron commander really excelled himself – it was as near Mach 1 as made no difference. Within minutes the word came by R/T – yet another telephoned complaint. 'Now we'll see,' said the OC Flying as he ground the gears on the Land Rover.

Nobody was really prepared for what they saw when the front door of the house was opened. There, bare and stark against the ceiling, was the empty frame of a chandelier, while on the carpet beneath was a neat pile of expensive-looking fragments! Yet nothing else ever got broken, just the long-suffering chandelier. Our unit was possibly unique in that it carried out these high-speed trials at low altitude, for there was a restriction in force preventing very high speeds below a certain height for the rest of the Service, in the interests of neighbourly behaviour.

In view of the present-day tendency for people to complain about almost anything, it was with some surprise that we observed the stoicism with which the local people accepted our activities; indeed, on certain occasions it must have seemed to them that we were going out of our way to be a confounded nuisance.

On rare occasions, events occurred that spread the load elsewhere, to the relief of the regulars, though to the discomfiture of others. On one such occasion I was required to air test a Scimitar that had had yaw damper trouble, and it was thought necessary to try this out eventually at high speed and low level before putting the aircraft back on trials strength.

It wasn't the best day in the world, with a cloudbase of 2,000 feet, but we needed the aeroplane, so I elected to fly at 1,500 feet, quite high by our standards. There was obviously some kind of resonant effect produced by the low and even cloudbase, because we had many reports of domestic breakages from many enraged householders, although I had not been at maximum speed.

One interesting case was at a farmhouse where some crockery had been broken, and when we sent an officer round to assess the damage with a view to payment, he found to his surprise that the only items broken in a dresser full of crockery were six teacups, which had been standing in a line. They had all shattered completely, leaving only a pathetic line of china bases surrounded by a profusion of broken best china! Yet a similar line of coffee cups were completely intact.

There is still a great deal we do not know about the resonant effects of noise, and the small amount of information that we accidentally gathered in passing is only a pointer to the results that are now being achieved, for good as well as ill, in industry and medicine, as well as in the field of future combat. The old Biblical story of the walls that came 'tumbling down' in Jericho was the direct result of a particular sound. Doesn't it make you wonder what sort of a noise that could have been, all those years ago?

23

In mid-Channel the cloud cleared, and there, below us, flitting across the water, was the black silhouette of our machine, just like the old aircraft recognition charts.

Nach England Gehen

I F anybody else had told me that they had just bought a Heinkel III from Spain and please would I go and get it, I would have suspected a leg-pull, but when the question was asked by Doug Arnold, who has already amassed a respectable private air force at Blackbushe, I realised that I was in for the experience of a lifetime. It transpired that the aeroplane was one of the machines that had been used for the film *Battle of Britain*, and had been fitted out as an executive transport. It had been maintained in flying condition, and since the date of the sale had done no flying, although the Merlins had been run regularly. The CAA had issued a temporary C of A to allow the machine to be collected from Torrejon, and all the aircraft papers, including export paperwork, were in order. It all seemed too good to be true, as if picking up Second World War bombers from Spain was an everyday occurrence. Peter Hoar, of British Caledonian, had done much of the groundwork, and was to fly with me, for which purpose he had equipped himself with a Bayside portable radio, just in case.

We assembled one evening at Blackbushe, six all told, including the pilot of the Cessna 402 that was to be our conveyance to Madrid civil airport. It being Tuesday, we were advised by Doug to get a move on, as Thursday in Spain was a public holiday. By the time all the equipment was on board we must have been near our maximum all-up weight, if the take-off performance was anything to go by. Darkness soon fell, and I switched on the cabin light to study the He III Pilot's Notes that Peter handed to me. This brought the first problem: they were written in Spanish! Picking out words here and there, but relying mainly on the various schematic diagrams, I struggled to understand the systems. The hydraulic system made no sense at all, and there was one bit about the approach with half flap being 'muy peligrosso' – very dangerous. Charming, I thought; somebody is going to have to translate this – carefully. There were also references to 'curved ailerons', which completely stumped me. Overhead Nantes further perusal of the notes was interrupted by the announcement from the front end that an alternator had come off line and we were diverting to Bordeaux, but by the time we had landed and sorted ourselves out it was too late to partake of any French cuisine, so with Doug's warning of Spanish holidays ringing in our ears, we turned in early.

Next day saw good progress, and we arrived at Madrid mid-morning. This was where our troubles really started. Unless you have handling organised at Madrid, you've had it. It took us 2 hours just to get off the airport and meet our Spanish agent. This accomplished, we set off by taxi to the military airfield at Torrejon, only 20 minutes away in theory, but by the time our taxi driver had got us lost several times, it was nearly 2 o'clock in the afternoon before we reached the hangar – and there she was. I had seen a Heinkel only once before, but as she sat in the gloom of the hangar she seemed to exude malevolence – or was it only dim childhood memories of the Blitz? A small crowd of Spanish Air Force personnel soon gathered, including, mercifully, a Captain who could speak English.

Now we were in business, and I could find out about these 'curved ailerons' (the ailerons seemed conventional enough to look at). Not a bit of it. Apparently work had ceased at 1.30pm and it was not possible to tow the aircraft out of the hangar. Could we push it out then, we asked. Much too difficult, we were told. Trying another tack, I asked the Captain if he would be kind enough to explain the function of the various levers in the cockpit. He raised his hands in horror at this. It seemed that the Heinkel was a very dangerous aeroplane to fly; only one pilot (very old) knew anything about handling it; one needed a ground course of instruction, a cockpit briefing, a dual check, where were our parachutes, and wouldn't it be better to wait until Friday? Patiently I tried again to get him to translate the cockpit inscriptions for me, but to no avail. Perhaps shock treatment would work.

'All right,' I said, 'get me a trolley-acc, shove the aircraft outside, and I'll get in and go, with or without a briefing.'

'You British are crazy!' he screamed and disappeared, never to be seen again.

So much for the shock treatment. By this time the hangar doors were being closed, so we had to abandon our efforts for the day. Meantime I had seen enough of the cockpit with its curious controls to know that I wasn't going anywhere until this lot had been thoroughly explained to me. Our agent disappeared to contact his friend, the General, as otherwise we were

stuck for yet another day, so we despondently made our way to the local
hotel, where I spent several fairly fruitless hours investigating the question of
'curved ailerons'. It appeared that there was some mechanism for drooping
them, but it was all very confusing; what I really needed was a proper
briefing. Then I had a bright idea. The erstwhile world aerobatic champion,
Tom Castanos, lived in Madrid, and we had known each other for many
years. It was worth a try. As luck would have it, he was off-duty from his
normal job of DC9 captain with Iberia, and only too pleased to help. Not
only was it great to meet him again, but it turned out that he had been a test
pilot at Torrejon and had flown the Heinkel many years ago.

Even Tom had trouble with the Pilot's Notes. It seemed that it was a
translation from the old Luftwaffe notes, and there were many mistakes. The
mysterious 'curved ailerons' turned out to be the flaps! As we progressed, it
became apparent why the Captain had been so concerned. On finals, it said,
don't let the slip ball get off centre, nor let the bank exceed 30 degrees. Also
use the controls very smoothly. Finally the landing was considered to be
rather hairy. With Tom's assistance, and with the many cockpit photographs
in the book, I was eventually fairly happy, and for the first time we could
relax and enjoy a meal, especially when word came through that the General
had authorised the base to open and let us out – on a Spanish holiday! Our
agent, it seemed, had some pull in high circles.

On our way to the field next day we had another bright idea. Both Peter
and I had military (RAF) flying suits; mine even had rank tabs. In spite of the
stifling heat, we put them on. As we got out of the car, the sentry crashed to
attention – and this in Spain, on a holiday! Things were looking up! Whether
it was the General, or the flying suits, or both, we never knew, but today
cooperation was in order. A Warrant Officer arrived to supervise things, and
as he obviously knew the aircraft I grabbed him, and with the help of the
agent got him to explain the function of the cockpit controls. With Tom's
briefing it all began to make sense. The undercarriage lever was equipped
with a tiny silver padlock to prevent any mishaps, but where was the key? A
search revealed a small leather pouch attached to the cockpit wall, and out
came several feet of silver chain with a key on the end of it! Unlike the
bomber version, where the control column can be unlocked and swung over
to the second pilot's position, this machine came with dual controls.

I spent a lot of time making sure I understood the fuel transfer system
because the engines feed directly from the inboard tanks and have to be kept

topped up from the outboards. Any mistakes and one can get into severe trouble with fuel asymmetry, spillage, or even running an inboard tank dry. The engine master cocks also controlled the oil supply to the engines, and there is a fuselage oil tank so that one can pump oil to either engine by hand. One can also use the oil from a failed engine to supply the good one. The various methods of lowering the undercarriage were also explained, but I was slightly disappointed to learn that the final method used on the bomber version was not fitted – a large cable cutter that sliced the main cable in half, allowing the gear to free fall!

Since we had to go to Madrid civil airport to clear customs, we made our tortuous way to the USAF base on the south side to flight plan, using the Spanish facilities there. We had been told to expect trouble, but our flying suits seemed to ease the way.

This was it! We fired up the ancient eight-channel VHF and asked for start-up; surprisingly the reply came back loud and clear, but we were told that we could not fly VFR to the civil airport, though it was only about 4 miles away and the weather was perfect. Perspiring freely under the Perspex of the glasshouse nose, and cursing all controllers, we disembarked and made for the hangar phone.

'If we can't fly VFR,' I said, 'why the hell did you accept the flight plan?'

'You must file IFR,' was the reply, 'and you must have a transponder.'

This was a great help, since (1) we had no transponder, (2) we were equipped with one dubious eight-channel radio plus the portable, and (3) our C of A said VFR only.

'How about special VFR?' I asked, but the answer was negative. 'How, then, do we get to Madrid?' I asked.

'You can't,' was the reply.

Impasse. By now we at least had the Test Centre on our side and sympathetic. 'Why don't you go via Zaragoza?' they said. This was reasonable, since it didn't really matter which airport we cleared through, so back we went to file a new flight plan. Any difficulties or 'muy peligrosso' areas had by now been forgotten in the struggle to get permission to leave. We also fuelled her to the gunwales, with fistfuls of pesetas rapidly changing hands. At least we could reach England in one hop, if necessary. There was no way they were going to let us back in once we were airborne.

At last we were ready. Frantic signals from the ground were eventually translated as 'You have not switched on the horizon'! First things first, I thought, let's start the engines. Ignoring all attempts by the groundcrew to persuade us to join them in a state of panic, we started the Merlins. At least this was a familiar area, and what a sweet pair of engines! By the time the trolley-acc and chocks were removed, the groundcrew were in a fine state of agitation, leaping up and down and waving their arms in a series of incomprehensible signals. The last I saw was the Warrant Officer indicating that I still had the sliding canopy open, which I obviously knew about since I was using it to give him a thumbs-up! The Cessna crew later told us that he was certain we were heading to our doom; I really couldn't understand the fuss, until I learned later that the Heinkel is supposed to be a very tricky machine. I reckon it was a rumour put about by Heinkel pilots to stop others from flying it!

The first problem area we encountered was the brakes, which are hydraulic but with no servo assistance. At the holding point it took both of us all our strength to restrain the aeroplane against 1,000rpm, since there is no parking brake. Later I found the best method of taxiing was to use large bursts of power to steer, but this is a technique that needs practice. With a non-steerable tailwheel, I lined up carefully. 'Make a right turn within 1 mile,' said the controller, and we were cleared to go. The only other twin-Merlin aeroplane I had flown was the Mosquito, so with this in mind I opened up cautiously to 1kg/sq cm, 'Sobreal Presion', which in Merlin language is +14 boost. I had mentally labelled the boost gauges to allow us to work in old-fashioned standard units, so .65 became +9, etc. At 3,000rpm the noise was unbelievable, and by the time I realised that she wasn't going to swing, she had lifted off, at 130km/h, slow and gentle, but very heavy on the controls. I selected gear up, and set the hydraulic selector to 'undercarriage'. This has the function of supplying pressure to either gear or flaps, but not both together. As I changed hands to throttle back to +9 and 2,850rpm, the selector jumped back to 'flaps'. A swift twist of the trim wheel and I changed hands again to select 'undercarriage'.

By now the speed was getting up and we had to stay at low level to avoid the Madrid traffic. 'Turn right' from the controller as I released the selector to throttle back further, whereupon it jumped back to 'flaps'. 'Your gear is still down,' said the tower, as if I didn't know. Peter, who could do nothing at this stage, had to watch me trying to carry out a five-handed operation, eventually having to hold the selector firmly to 'undercarriage' while the hydraulic system screamed its displeasure. Acceleration was slow, but steady, and I eventually throttled back to +4 so that I could get the gear to lock up. As it did so the selector returned to 'flaps' with a bang that nearly amputated a finger, the hydraulic system screaming continuously. This racket only stopped when I selected flaps up, the roar of the Merlins seeming peaceful by comparison. 'You're clear this frequency – good day,' said the tower, which normally produces a flurry of maps and charts in the cockpit. On this occasion we switched off the radio and heaved a sigh of relief – we were airborne at last. With the radiator shutters in 'auto' the temperatures were well within limits, and we settled down at 4,000 feet over the featureless terrain. The view, especially downward, was incredible, though we felt like a tomato in a greenhouse.

... we switched off the radio and heaved a sigh of relief – we were airborne at last.

Now that we were clear of Madrid our ancient VHF set was not much use, so I put on a flying helmet to keep the noise out, leaving Peter to raise Zaragoza on the portable set. This set would only support one set of earphones, so he was promoted to chief radio operator. By this time the machine was trimmed out and running sweetly, though heading changes were a major operation. The ailerons were powerful enough, the only problem being the strength required to move them. Adverse aileron yaw was extremely high, and one really had to stand on the rudder to initiate a turn. I reckon that 2 hours is as much as anybody can take, and Peter occasionally had to take over to give me a rest. The nearest I can get to describing it in relation to handling a light aircraft is to imagine a giant, twin-engined Puss Moth. By now we were rattling along at 280km/h using +4 and 2,400rpm, which gave 250 litres per hour per engine. We even began to enjoy it, and our cup of happiness was complete when Peter raised Zaragoza on the portable radio. Now for the 'muy peligrosso' bit!

It wasn't until I throttled back that I realised how clean this aeroplane was. The speed decay was very slow, and I remembered that an early Rolls-Royce engine had been tested in a Heinkel 70, which was very much like the He III in appearance; indeed, some historians say that the Spitfire wing was based on the elliptical wing of the Heinkel. Whatever the truth of this, the elliptical wing approaches aerodynamic perfection and makes the He III a very efficient flying machine. Once again I had my five-handed act, in reverse, and we were soon settled on finals, with no appreciable trim changes from either gear or flaps.

Flying the original Bomber Command approach, I drove it carefully in from about 3 miles. Concentrating hard, I slowly flattened out and started to throttle back. I was aware of a soft, steady rhythmic jolting – what was this? Then it dawned on me – we were down, to the best landing I've ever made! Far from being 'muy peligrosso', she was easy and forgiving, a bit like a DC3 to land, but with a typical soft German undercarriage that makes sprog pilots feel a bit of an ace. But of course it couldn't last. As we taxied in, standing with all my weight on the right brake, the Heinkel had obviously taken a dislike to three Learjets on the apron and was ominously bearing down upon them. Peter was already calculating the enormity of the insurance claim when I remembered that these were only glorified car brakes, so I started to pump them, and sure enough, the nose started to swing round, albeit reluctantly. I swear I saw the Learjets flinch! The airport was alive with holidaymakers dressed in all their finery, so we must have looked a desperate and disreputable pair in our sweat-stained flying suits.

Here the story was different: everyone was helpful and we were turned round and cleared in no time. Iberia provided a trolley-acc, and incredibly refused to accept any payment, with the remark that 'Flying that thing you deserve all the support you can get.' Carefully avoiding the Learjets (by now I had found how to taxi on engines), we cautiously made our way to the holding point and, with increasing confidence, roared off on the next leg to Bordeaux, retracting gear and flaps with the usual shrieks of protest from the hydraulics – I know I shall never get used to that noise! With some misgivings I experimented with transfer cocks and pumps, and was mildly surprised when the fuel went where it was supposed to, but one still has to be careful where one leaves the cocks, because there is no 'off' position, and one has to leave the system so that it is in a closed circuit to prevent inadvertent transfer. Signs of jubilation from the right-hand seat indicated two-way R/T contact with Bordeaux, and we were soon rolling down the runway. One of the controllers rushed out to the aircraft, and my fast thought was, 'What have we done wrong now?'

'Mon Dieu!' he said. 'With a radio as bad as that, I knew it had to be something interesting!'

By this time we were somewhat dehydrated, so we retired to the bar to await the arrival of the Cessna, which to our great surprise had not preceded us. It later turned out that it had taken him no less than 4 hours to get out of Madrid airport! Just as well we didn't go there with the Heinkel – we would still have been there!

With a decent night's sleep we felt ready for the leg to Gatwick and, although reluctant to leave the hospitable atmosphere of Bordeaux, there was an air of excitement as we climbed aboard; it seemed that we really were going to get there after all.

It was a perfect day for flying, and the old Heinkel droned on steadily, the quiet pattern of the French countryside flowing in a panoramic stream below the transparent nose. Stratus over the Channel made us drop down, and we wondered what the occupants of the odd fishing boats thought, as if the clock had been turned back 35 years. In mid-Channel the cloud cleared, and there, below us, flitting across the water, was the black silhouette of our machine, just like the old aircraft recognition charts.

As we approached Gatwick we finally achieved two-way contact on our eight-channel set, and were cleared No 1 to finals. The aircraft is so clean that one is tempted to use the full 60 degrees of available flap, but I kept it down to 45 degrees and flew a flatter approach, just in case I needed to overshoot. The trim change with power and speed is quite high, though gear and flap have no particular effect, other than a marked ballooning when the flaps go down. Lateral control is very poor on the approach and some strenuous work on the rudder is called for to pick up a dropping wing.

With a lot of interesting eyes looking on I elected to do a wheel landing, which used up quite a bit of runway. There was a rather curious complaint from the tower that I had not flown in formation with the Cessna, an operation in which I had no particular interest at that stage. The Heinkel is such a clean aeroplane that even with throttles closed I would have overtaken the Cessna on the approach. When flying old aeroplanes such as the He III one has to stay flexible and keep the safety of the operation in the forefront of one's mind, regardless of specific procedures.

On the last leg we were able to take some pictures from the Cessna, after which, with the shortest runway of the trip in front of us, I took her up to 5,000 feet for a couple of stalls, but not before we called Farnborough and declared ourselves to be a 'Rolls-powered One-Eleven out of Gatwick', and would they like an overfly? This resulted in people almost falling out of office windows in an attempt to get a better view. ATC Farnborough is always helpful and likes to see strange aeroplanes, so we were glad to oblige. The stalling tests gave us the biggest surprise of the trip. Reluctant to lose speed in the clean configuration, she gave the impression of a big fish sliding through a silent pool. Quiet, steady, streamlined, gradually she slowed. Ready for anything, we waited. Just before the stall, the stick had to be pulled back a little faster, until at 155km/h the nose dropped very gently. I pulled the stick fully back, but she took no notice; the nose continued going down and she started to fly again. I had never seen such a viceless aeroplane. With wheels down and 45-degree flap the behaviour was identical, with a stall speed of 135km/h. I could not provoke any other response. Peter and I looked at each other in amazement – what ladylike behaviour! Though slow to roll into a turn, she pivoted on a wingtip with 60-degree bank just like a Tiger Moth, with no fuss at all. But eventually we had to go down. Two low runs for the cameras, and I let her settle in a three-point landing. In that short time we had become very fond of her; she was a classic-handling aeroplane, one of the old school. She was certainly not 'muy peligrosso'!

24

I am no longer aware of the crowd as a collection of people; whether I fly for one person or 100,000 the display will be the same.

The Big Show

'**A**ND now, ladies and gentlemen, look to your right over the black sheds…' Familiar words to those thousands who make the bi-annual pilgrimage to that Mecca of aeronautical gatherings, Farnborough, and the SBAC display.

How many of the spectators must wonder what it is like to demonstrate one's aircraft in front of such a vast audience, on a stage of such gigantic proportions? The performers follow each other with parade-ground precision, the machines sweep by, regal, effortless, or in a blur of speed, reheat blazing, a Wagnerian crescendo of thunder.

It all starts with the briefing, in the superficially casual atmosphere of the Pilots' Tent. Voices are hushed, the tinkle of cutlery and the scraping of chairs fades, and all attention is on the OC Flying, who bears total responsibility for the smooth running of the display. Each of us has a programme giving take-off times and display duration. I scan my sheet – 'Falcon, take-off 1527 hours, 5 minutes'. I relax, because I have been allocated the display time I requested – a last-minute change could wreak havoc with my planned sequence.

Now the duty meteorologist reads out the forecast – no problem today, so we can expect the full display from all pilots. Air Traffic briefing is next, giving us details we already know, but nothing here is left to chance. Finally the OC Flying has a few words to say on the expected standard of flying from all, and a reminder that safety is paramount.

We synchronise watches. With the briefing over, the buzz of voices breaks out again as pilots finish their lunch, queue for coffee and make their way out into the pilots' enclosure to watch the start of the display. The exceptions are the small groups who are to fly first. Their pace is quicker as they prepare to board the RAE taxi out to their aircraft.

I have more than an hour to wait, so I go over our routine with my colleague in the right-hand seat. We are lucky, for we have been able to get some practice in recent weeks. Far too often pilots have been required to perform with the bare minimum of practice time. Only their skill and experience has allowed them to do this, with the crowd none the wiser. We relax and watch the different styles and techniques of each performance. I study the approach of each pilot to the exacting task of presenting the best points of his aeroplane. There is always something to learn.

Well, chaps, time to go. We board the taxi and are whisked out to the Falcon. The French mechanic is fussing over it, trying to improve on the already 100% serviceability. We are carrying minimum safe fuel to give us the maximum in performance, and I brief the mechanic to stand by with chocks after we land, because I am going to use the brakes – hard!

Concorde makes its flypast, dead on time, and this is our prearranged cue to start engines. We listen out on R/T, but say nothing. Here at Farnborough we have probably the best and most efficient use of R/T anywhere. Any other system would result in chaos. Now, as the Jaguar roars across the field we note the One-Eleven at the marshalling point, and make our R/T call – 'Falcon, taxi'. The reply is equally brief – 'Falcon, hold at Alpha'. This clears us as far as the arrester runway, behind the One-Eleven.

As the bigger airliner starts its take-off run, ATC calls 'Falcon, holding point'. We do not acknowledge, but roll forward and hold just short of the Runway 25 threshold. The R/T is silent now as we complete our checks, leaving the pressurisation off to increase performance. 'One-Eleven, 30 seconds' from the tower, and I see the airliner turning short finals for landing. I tighten my shoulder straps and receive a confirmatory nod from the co-pilot. Owing to the control wheel's smooth surface I am wearing cape leather gloves – we cannot risk a hand slipping here.

The One-Eleven sweeps past and touches down for a maximum-performance landing. 'Falcon line-up' from ATC – we taxi into position. Now things are going to happen fast. I open up to 1.2 EPR – from here I can achieve rapid acceleration. As the One-Eleven clears the runway I start increasing power. The engines are winding up fast – 'Falcon, clear to go'. I release the brakes and bang the stopwatch. 'Full power' calls the co-pilot, who will monitor engines continuously from now on. Acceleration is high, and at 80 knots I transfer on to the rudder. Approaching 100 knots I push forward slightly to compress the nose leg, using the rebound to help me I make a snatch pull, which I check immediately. The nose wheels leap off the ground and as the aircraft reaches its optimum angle I apply right aileron.

Now the left wheels are off the ground as we reach flying speed – no Vr or V2 here. Our performance is not as high as some of the other aircraft, so we must use a climbing turn off the runway to give the illusion of higher performance. Airborne, and I call 'gear up' as we continue to accelerate, just over the wood on the north side of the runway.

Airspeed 130, 140, 150 – that's fast enough, and I call for 1.2 EPR again. Fifty degrees of bank; I am holding exactly 2 'g' on our borrowed accelerometer taped to the top coaming. This is the limit for 15-degree flap and I need maximum 'g' for our minimum-radius turn, well inside the airfield. Now the crowd is in view through the windscreen as we complete 270 degrees of turn. 'Undercarriage red lights still on,' from the co-pilot – I acknowledge. The 'g' load has prevented the undercarriage from locking up. 'Approaching safety line,' from the right seat – this is the line we are not allowed to cross in the interests of crowd safety. It is clearly marked by a series of dayglo strips on the ground, parallel to the runway and on the north side of it.

Position is good, one-third of the way down the crowd line, as I reverse the bank using full aileron. During the reversal I release the 'g' and delay commencing the left turn as I flash a glance at the undercarriage indicator. Two thumps from the belly and the lights go out, but now I am very close to the safety line as I pull hard into the turn. The stall warning squeaks at me so I ease off slightly – better to infringe the line by a few feet than to pull into stall warning. But no, we are clear and as we turn away I call for full power – again we need the illusion of thrust by making as much noise as possible with our jet pipes aimed at the crowd. But this is a quiet aeroplane – we cannot drown the Lightnings' roar! Besides noise, we now need all the performance we can get as I pull up, holding 2 'g' all the while into a climbing turn, which I now start to reverse. The crowd is somewhere behind my starboard tailplane as I start the right turn back, still climbing, with 15-degree flap.

Squeezing every inch of height I can get, I roll on 90-degree bank and call for flaps in – if I have judged this right the flaps and leading edges will lock in just before I reach their limiting speed of 200 knots. Yes, all lights out as the nose drops, still with full power. Two minutes 15 seconds on the watch and now the co-pilot calls the turn – 'Ease it … tighten up … hold it there' – a running commentary, for I still cannot see from the left-hand seat as we come in from the crowd's right for a high-speed run. I would have preferred to do this downwind, but it just wouldn't fit into the 5-minute programme without losing position or degenerating into a series of flypasts.

The speed increases to 350 knots. She swings a little wide – a warning from the co-pilot as we approach the safety line and the accelerometer quivers on the red line as I tighten the turn. Already as we near the half-way mark of the display I am perspiring. I am trimming hard, but the stick forces are changing fast; I hold the wheel firmly and now I can see the runway, the crowd, we're OK on the safety line. I ease down low over the black sheds; now we're really moving, and as we flash across the tower I call 'cut', and the co-pilot slams both throttles closed. With a thin, high whistle, the Falcon streaks across the field. 'Airbrakes – now.' As I roll her fast into a vertically banked turn away, the co-pilot selects airbrakes.

The whistle instantly becomes a rumble. I lift the nose to assist deceleration. Up in a climbing spiral, tight inside the field, watching the fast falling airspeed, trimming back hard, and in quick succession 'Flaps 15 – gear down – full flap'. Still with the airbrakes out, the aircraft hangs suspended at 4,000 feet. I keep the nose down and the turn going – the rate of descent is colossal as I steep turn in the dive, all inside the field. The vibration is high with airbrakes out, now I am in trim, I call for 1.2 EPR and listen to the engines winding up – no time to look into the cockpit now. I have one hand on the airbrake lever, watch the descent rate, watch the safety line, and as we swing out of our turn we are towards the crowd.

I select airbrakes in, call, 'My throttles, landing light on.' Now as we near the end of the display I need varied throttle openings so I will operate them myself. 'Falcon, 1 minute' from ATC. Tail on to the crowd and I call for landing light off. Nearly finished, but don't rush this last bit. I mustn't go too far downwind or the impact of the display will be lost, but if I don't go far enough I will not be able to get rid of my speed, and I want this to be a short landing.

To keep the crowd's attention I select airbrakes out again; this lets me use more power and make more noise. People never look at a quiet aeroplane unless it is right in front of them. Now I lift the nose really high, with full power against airbrake as I make a high wingover to the right. 'Thirty seconds' from the tower, but now I am on finals, throttling back, with the airbrakes giving me a very high and hopefully spectacular descent. In service one is not allowed to land with airbrakes out, but this is a display.

Fifteen seconds to go as the black sheds slip past below, 1.2 Vs, really slow, held in the air by thrust, I can feel that we are on the reverse side of the drag curve. Don't flare, let her fly on. Speed steady at 100 knots as she hits the ground, exactly on the line in front of the President's Tent. Nosewheels down, and full brake! With all my strength I stand on the pedals. She is not an STOL aircraft, but it was a brave attempt!

We clear the runway 2 seconds inside our time and are grateful to open the direct vision window to let in some air. I stopcock the right engine so that I do not need to use the brakes; they need time to cool down.

Now we can relax; it's all over until tomorrow, as the F.28 sweeps overhead on its display. Our smiling mechanic is waiting for us with chocks as we arrive in dispersal, our car is there to take us back to the Pilots' Tent. The Falcon's brakes are barely warm.

An exacting task, which must be repeated six times, flying to the limits of the aeroplane, never outside them. And so many things to consider – positioning, the safety line, timing, wind, sun, even the displays put on by the pilots before and after. Positioning is perhaps the hardest to achieve, and yet when this is really perfect nobody notices, because they are not given cause to think about it.

With a jet aeroplane one can display to a long crowd line. On the public days, however, we have a small problem. This comes in the shape of a Pitts Special single-seat competition biplane that I have been asked to fly. It will not be possible to present a close-knit display to the whole length of the crowd, so I have decided to give a demonstration of a freestyle international competition sequence, orientated precisely on the President's Tent.

This time my briefing is more personal and I am given an operations order clearly stating my permitted display limits. I will have to modify my final manoeuvre to parallel the crowd line, instead of straight at the judge, as would be the case in an aerobatic contest.

Perhaps in the Falcon I was a little concerned about demonstrating a jet aeroplane among similar types flown by more experienced jet display pilots. In the Pitts Special I am at home, I am relaxed and confident. I have no radio so I wait on the grass near the tower, with the sun glittering on the idling propeller. My straps are rock hard, all seven of them, my altimeter is set to minus 100 feet – which helps compensate for altimeter lag – and windscreen and goggles are polished. Fuel and smoke oil contents are maximum, and the programme card is clipped securely to the panel.

A green light from the tower. I taxi out slowly, the tiny machine jerking and jolting on the coarse concrete. I line up in front of the President's Tent and look at the crowd – I am looking up at them! The commentator's voice is plainly audible, booming over the loudspeaker system. I am no longer distant and isolated in a jet-propelled aluminium cylinder – this feels more like an airshow!

Again a green light, 2,000rpm, the engine sounds clean, start the watch, release brakes, full throttle and smoke on. The crowd, from being amused at the tiny biplane, dwarfed by even the Gnats, now stand riveted by its incredible performance, but I am oblivious to them – I have a preplanned task to perform. The tail is up, the wheels are drumming on the smoother asphalt of the runway; smoke, white and evil-smelling, billows into the cockpit, the moan of the wires rises and blends with the note of the engine. She is dancing and bucking. So I let her come off the ground, and hold her low. She is accelerating nearly four times faster than the Falcon, and at 120mph I rotate to 45 degrees.

Like an arrow the machine shoots upwards, a ruler-straight smoke trail marking our path. Now we can be sure the crowd will pay attention! Smoke off at 1,500 feet and I complete my pre-aerobatic checks as I settle into my climb pattern. This is regulated so that I fly three sides of a square, assessing wind drift on each one to check on the Met forecast. I also time my rate of climb to confirm full performance. If there is any significant deterioration I will abandon and land – I will take no chances.

Ninety seconds from brakes off I am curving in towards the crowd at a height of 1,000 metres (although the altimeter is in feet, in contest work we think in metres). I am no longer aware of the crowd as a collection of people; whether I fly for one person or 100,000 the display will be the same. My display time is 15 seconds away as I gauge my intended dive line. Altitude, viewing angle, wind drift, aircraft visual density, position and seconds to go – all these parameters are being monitored. Zero minus 12 seconds, the optimum Pitts diving time, and I drop a wing and let her fall into the dive.

I stare through the windscreen – the President's Tent is centred in the cabane struts, a small white square, rapidly expanding. Smoke on, the engine noise and the scream of the wires are blotted out by the howl of the now supersonic propeller blades. I have no doubt that every eye is on the hurtling Pitts. Maximum speed, the whole machine is vibrating, the controls iron hard against the slipstream, throttle back a bit, keep out of the vibration range, zero minus 3, 2, 1 – now I press back on the stick, bracing hard against the rapidly rising 'g', vertical, check and instantly snap through 45 degrees with Guards precision, and again, and again, eight in all, holding pitch and yaw rock steady all the while in a vertical eight-point climbing roll.

Hold the vertical line, the speed has gone, keep her straight with right rudder against the thrashing propeller – now! Full left rudder and she cartwheels into a stall turn. A four-point diving roll and hard back into level flight, shuddering on the edge of a high-speed stall. Time gone, 25 seconds, I also note that the first figure was exactly above the safety line. Racing away from the President's Tent I delay my next pull up by 1 second; this will place me comfortably 150 to 200 feet beyond the safety line. I will creep in again as I get lower.

Over the top of a half outside loop with the time exactly right as I change into the main axis to display parallel to the safety line. Height is good – I have 50 metres in hand – but as there is no turbulence I decide not to conserve this, but to trade it for more speed and bigger manoeuvres. This means I must progress more quickly through the routine so I must squeeze the sequence tighter around the centre. Good, I can cut half a second off the gap between each successive figure. Into a 45-degree dive, throttle back, wait for the precise speed – and go! A one-and-a-half-turn positive flick-roll, almost too fast for the eye to follow, but I know the timing I need to stop this one on line. One minute and 5 seconds as I go up into the outside avalanche, dead on centre. On the way down I note that there is a slight northerly component to the wind at this altitude, which will drift me in towards the safety line as I get lower. It's my lucky day!

Now I have settled into the routine, my flying has smoothed out, I am no longer aware of the crowd, only the safety line and the President's Tent. Timing is running well within 1 second of ideal as I progress into the composite manoeuvres. They look difficult, and without the commentator most of them would be lost on the crowd, but he is a very experienced aerobatic pilot and he has a copy of my programme in front of him, with timings included. He doesn't actually have to look up, for he knows I will fly the programme precisely, and he is keeping just a few seconds ahead of me, preparing the crowd for the next manoeuvre.

Now I am at the bottom height limit of 100 metres (328 feet). This is the international height limit and I will not come below it in the freestyle performance. But I have speed, and I can play the yo-yo, trading speed for height and back again. Position is again critical as I approach centre, with 3 minutes 45 seconds gone, and now I change back on to the 'B' axis with a downward 270-degree flick-roll, pulling out tail to the crowd. Straight into a 270-degree rolling circle, this is a fast figure. Normally it would take 25 seconds, and I have allowed myself 12. It must be perfectly coordinated, rolling 4 degrees for every 1 degree of turn. The circle must be a helix in the air, to make a true circle over the ground. The roll and turn rates must be constant, and I must not gain or lose a foot of height. Here, at a display, this would not really matter, but I will not accept a lower standard.

The end of the circle puts me back again into the 'A' axis and I enter the final 40 seconds. The last manoeuvre I must angle so that it does not cause an infringement. Five seconds to go, I roll into knife-edge flight, 3 seconds and I hit the rudder. The Pitts flick-rolls wildly through 540 degrees and stops exactly in opposite knife-edge. A slight pause, then I snap the aircraft back to level flight. Five minutes – precisely.

I select smoke off. When the residual smoke has cleared I throttle back and slip quietly over the black sheds. My threshold speed is 100mph, only a fraction less than in the Falcon. I touch down, stop abeam the President's Tent, turn towards it in salute, and taxi clear.

Abruptly, it is over. All the planning, the preparation, the concentration, have culminated in this short 5-minute display. Three hundred seconds of time – and now it is finished. It will be two years before we can repeat it. With engine idling I taxi slowly back to the hangar, conscious again of the booming loudspeakers. As I switch off and listen to the commentator, the finality of this moment comes home to me – 'And now, ladies and gentlemen, look to your right over the black sheds...'

25

...for the first time the certainty that I was about to be killed came home to me.

Wing and a Prayer

OR the first time since the inception of the World Aerobatic Championships ten years before, it was decided to hold this event in the United Kingdom in 1970. The British Team, from quite modest beginnings, had grown over this period to a point where we stood a good chance of being highly placed, equipped as we were with two modern aircraft, a two-seater Zlin Trener, and a 160hp single-seater Zlin 526 Akrobat.

This latter machine was owned by a group of dedicated aerobatic pilots, and we had set ourselves a difficult target in forming the spearhead of the team that was to represent the UK. The airfield chosen for the 6th World Aerobatic Championships was RAF Hullavington, in Wiltshire, and at last we had one of the advantages of the home team, namely the ability to fly over the contest airfield for several months to familiarise ourselves with the local topography. Because Hullavington is in the Lyneham Zone, we had to maintain telephone communication with Lyneham at all times, and this meant that some of the aerobatic team had to man the otherwise disused control tower when flying was taking place. This suited us very well, because of the need to have somebody on the ground to criticise our performances, since errors of as little as 2 degrees in pitch or roll could lose valuable marks in the contest.

So it was that, on a fine June morning, I took off in the Zlin Akrobat to practice my freestyle sequence. The wind was very light, so did not pose any problem, but I was not quite satisfied with my first two rehearsals. I decided to try once again. This time things were progressing a little better, and I settled down to fly steadily. The aircraft was going beautifully, and I determined to finish the sequence then land, but as I pulled out of my fifth manoeuvre I ran into trouble. As the aircraft levelled out of the dive there was a loud bang and a severe jolt shook the machine; I was thrown sideways in the cockpit, and at the same instant there was a very loud and peculiar change in the slipstream noise.

The problem seemed to be on the left of the aircraft, but when I looked left everything seemed normal, except that I was being forced against the left side of the cockpit.

I throttled back instinctively and looked around, to find that although the left wing was flying straight and level, the rest of the aeroplane was rolling to the left, around the failure point in the left wing root.

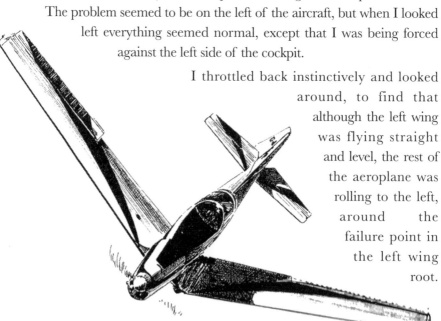

... there was a loud bang and a severe jolt shook the machine...

By this stage the aircraft was beginning to lose height, although I still had some degree of control remaining. I throttled back to reduce air loads but this caused the nose to drop further, and dihedral was by now noticeably increasing, and the roll and yaw to the left were becoming steadily more determined. I then tried full power in an attempt to get the nose up, but to no avail. By now I was outside the airfield and losing height fast. It was my intention to try and keep the wings as level as possible and to try and hit the ground at as shallow an angle as possible, hopefully in an open space.

It was soon apparent, however, that due to the rapid loss of control I was experiencing I was not going to make it, and for the first time the certainty that I was about to be killed came home to me. Control was finally lost at about 300 feet, when the aircraft had turned left through 90 degrees from the original heading, and was banked about 90 degrees to the left (at least the fuselage was). The left wing by now had folded to about 45 degrees and I was treated to the interesting spectacle of the rivets along the top of the main spar opening up like a zip fastener as dihedral increased. When the nose finally dropped I was holding full right aileron, full right rudder, and full power, with a large amount of sideslip. The natural tendency to pull back on the stick only made the situation worse.

In spite of being badly frightened I was still able to think clearly at this stage and I remembered a report I had heard many years ago about a Bulgarian pilot who had had a top wing bolt fail on an early mark of Zlin while under negative 'g', and that the aircraft had involuntarily flick-rolled the right way up, whereupon the wing came back into position, and the aircraft was landed by a very frightened, but alive, pilot. I had guessed by this time that a lower wing bolt had failed and that I was faced with a similar situation, albeit inverted.

It seemed that if positive 'g' had saved the Bulgarian, negative 'g' might work for me, though at this stage I was so low that I did not have much hope of success. Two things helped me: taking some positive action, no matter how hopeless, was preventing panic, and if it went wrong, at least it would be quick. Anyway there was no time left, and I couldn't think of anything else to try. I centralised the rudder, rolled left and pushed, still with full throttle. The wing snapped back into position instantly, with a loud bang that made me even more concerned for the structure. Immediately the negative 'g' started to rise and the nose started coming up, but I was too low: the trees ahead filled the windscreen, the throttle was wide open and I pushed the stick as far forward as I dared. For a split second the leaves and branches seemed to reach out at me, then they were gone and I was clear, climbing fast, inverted. Almost before I could appreciate my escape, the engine spluttered and died. Instinctively I eased back on the stick to glide inverted, while I searched frantically for the cause. Then I found it – fuel pressure zero. I checked the fuel cock and found it in the 'off' position. I had been thrown around in the cockpit at the moment the wing failed, and had probably knocked the cock off then. I selected the reserve fuel and immediately realised that this position would take fuel from the bottom of the gravity tank, which was of course now upside down. I quickly reselected main tank, and after a few coughs the engine picked up and ran at full power again.

... I pushed the stick as far forward as I dared.

By now I was quite low and was initially satisfied to climb straight ahead to 1,000 feet and to return to the airfield. The remainder of the team had been very quick off the mark and had alerted the crash vehicles as soon as they saw the wing starting to move. Meanwhile I throttled back to conserve fuel, as the Zlin has a maximum endurance of 8 minutes in inverted flight. I retrimmed for inverted flight, and steadied the stick between my knees while I used both hands to tighten my shoulder straps. There was no question of bailing out – I had no parachute. It was now that I had to fight against giving way to panic. I could not expect to survive this incident; indeed, at any time I expected the left wing to come off completely. There was an overwhelming temptation to stay airborne for the full 8 minutes, rather than attempt a landing earlier, thereby cutting my expected life span in half. At a time like this it is surprising how important an extra few minutes can be. I had to force myself to make the decision to try a landing – the question was, how? I considered using undercarriage or flaps, but rejected both. Flaps were no use to me while inverted, and I could not fly right way up anyway. Also if only one flap extended it would cause an immediate loss of control. The undercarriage required more thought. If I could make an inverted approach with a last-minute roll-out, I might be able to put the aircraft down on its wheels. However, if the gear fully or partially collapsed the aircraft might turn over. Perhaps the biggest argument against this was that the Zlin undercarriage usually locks down with a solid thump. I did not know exactly what damage had occurred and I was concerned in case the strain of lowering the wheels might remove the wing altogether. It was just as well that I left the wheels up, because the failure was not the wing bolt after all, but a fatigue failure in the centre section lower spar boom, inboard of the undercarriage leg attachment.

I also considered four possibilities for landing, namely inverted ditching, deliberately crashing inverted into trees to take the impact, inverted crash-landing on the airfield, or an inverted approach with a last-minute roll-out for a belly landing.

The last seemed to hold the best chances for survival, but I then decided to experiment to see which way was the best to roll out; if the rate of fold of the wing was sufficiently slow it might have been possible to exercise some control over the proposed landing. A roll-out to the left was attempted, whereupon the wing immediately folded again. As gently as possible I eased negative 'g' on again, but the wing still came back into position with a solid bang, and as the speed rose in the ensuing dive I could see the whole wing moving slightly. The wing attachments seemed to be getting weaker, so I decided against further experiments; the next attempt would be the real thing at low altitude. Common sense told me that the whole thing was impossible, but I had to try. At least as long as I kept thinking, I was able to control panic. Indeed, as one close shave followed another there was less of a tendency to panic; it seemed that the mind could only accept so much in the way of fright, and by the time I had flown a wide inverted circuit and positioned the aircraft on finals, I was concentrating so hard that there was no room for fear.

I was aiming for the grass, parallel to the main runway; there was no wind to speak of. The temptation to stay in the air until the fuel was exhausted was still strong, but I determined to stick to my decision. If I got it wrong, I would need that fuel to overshoot and try again. I left the canopy on; I didn't know if the handling would be much affected if I jettisoned it, and also I didn't want my height judgement affected by slipstream – this approach had to be exactly right. I crossed the boundary of the aerodrome slightly high, at 200 feet, at 180km/h with the throttle closed. I slowly levelled the aeroplane as low as I dared, then at 140km/h I rolled hard to the right, opening up to full power at the same time, and holding just enough negative 'g' in a slight outside barrel roll to keep the wing in place. The axis of the roll was the left wingtip, which left a furrow through the grass for 36 feet, without breaking the plastic cover on the navigation light. By a combination of good judgement, and incredible luck, I had got it right!

As the wings started to level, the nose was down due to the barrel roll, and to ease the impact I pulled back hard on the stick and cut the throttle. The good wing eased the fall, against hard aileron, but the left wing folded straight up, though not

...the left wingtip left a furrow through the grass for 36 feet...

before the rate of descent had been slightly reduced. With a bang like the end of the world she hit the ground hard. As the controls went slack I released them and tried to curl up into a ball, knees and feet pulled up and in, and head down protected by arms. The aircraft careered across the grass, the left wing bouncing and flapping like a wounded bird, then with a final jolt everything stopped. I couldn't believe it – I was still alive! Then another thought occurred – the petrol tanks had split! To have survived that experience only to burn spurred me into action. I struggled for long seconds to release the double safety harness only to find the canopy jammed! I gave it a resounding blow and it flew open, and as I scrambled out onto the broken wing I felt quite surprised that I was still mobile – I half expected to discover broken bones, but I was only bruised. I looked back at the Zlin, broken, never to fly again, and marvelled at my escape. I sat on the grass and realised how all my senses had been heightened by the drama of the last few minutes – the colour of the grass and sky, the smell of the earth, the song of birds. Never before or since has it been so clear.

We heard from the manufacturer a couple of weeks later. They sent a telegram that summed it all up in three words: 'Sorry – congratulations – thanks'! They also let us use their factory demonstrator, a Zlin 526F with 180hp, which I flew into fifth place in the World Championships. But my real victory had been weeks before, in the old 160hp Zlin Akrobat, where the prize was – life.

PHOTOGRAPH REFERENCES

All, photographs are courtesy of the William's family archive unless otherwise credited

Centre colour photo section:

i   Neil flying Spitfire IXb MH434. This is perhaps the Spitfire most closely associated with Williams. MH343 is still flying in the hands of The Old Flying Machine Company, based at Duxford.

Neil Williams at the controls of Lancaster NX611.

ii   Cosmic Wind G-ARUL photographed at Redhill in the 1970s. Redhill was the home of the Tiger Club from 1959 to 1990. *Ken Ellis Collection*

Neil at the controls of the Shuttleworth Collection Sopwith Pup, identifiable here from the elevated position of the Vickers gun (this Pup was re-configured from a Sopwith Dove, a two-seat conversion). Other differences from the St. Cyrien Pup are the slightly shorter main undercarriage and steeper fin leading-edge angle.

iii   Meteor TT.20 WM167 pictured at Blackbushe in April 1976. *Ken Ellis Collection*

A close-up portrait of Yak 11 G-AYAK. Neil's son, David, is just visible in the rear cockpit.

iv   CASA-built He 111. This aircraft is believed to have been the last CASA 2.111 in active service with the Spanish Air Force, it is now preserved at the Cavanaugh Flight Museum in Texas.

Broken Zlin Z526 G-AWAR at Hullavington, June 1970.

Photograph Information & credit

Page 156   Single Seat Tiger Moth G-AOAA 'The Deacon', photographed at Redhill in June 1977. *Air Team Images*

Page 162   Sea Fury G-BCOW Blackbushe in the 1970s. *John Bell*

Page 164   Sea Fury G-BCOW at Blackbushe, April 1976 *Ken Ellis Collection*

Page 168   Sea Fury G-BCOW photographed at Strathallan Air Day 14th July 1979 *John Bell*

Page 171   A Supermarine Scimitar F1 of the Royal Aircraft Establishment. *Tony Buttler*

Page 177   Neil studying handling notes for the CASA He III.

Page 185   Heinkel crew, left to right: Bob Diver; Neil Williams, Peter Hoar – engineer and British Caledonian Captain. This photograph taken at Strathallan by the then manager, Dick Richardson. *Dick Richardson*

Page 193   Pitts S-1S G-AZPH being flown by Neil Williams. Note the Welsh Dragon emblem carried on the fin. As with all British Team aircraft the colour scheme was designed by Neil's brother Lynn Williams, who also produced the drawings in this book. Neil flew this aircraft to fourth place in the World Aerobatics Championship in Kiev in 1976.

   G-AZPH is now hanging in the Science Museum, London.

Page 195   Zlin 526 G-AWAR in knife-edge flight

Page 201   Neil Williams with Zlin-G-AWAR at Hullavington following his remarkable crash-landing on 3rd June 1970. Williams was subsequently awarded the Queen's Commendation for Valuable Service in the Air for this amazing feat of airmanship.

   Williams' own logbook entry of the flight reads:

   "STRUCTURAL FAILURE. LEFT WING FOLDED. INVERTED APPROACH AND SUCCESSFUL CRASH LANDING ON A/F"

   Neil was in the air again before the end of the day, flying a Stampe from Hullavington to Booker (Wycombe Air Park). His logbook entry for that flight reads:

   "RELIEF TO BE AIRBORNE AGAIN. LOOP EN ROUTE JUST FOR THE HELL OF IT."

ABBREVIATIONS:

ADF	Automatic Direction Finding
AOC	Air Operators Certificate
APU	Auxiliary Power Unit
ASI	Air Speed Indicator
ATC	Air Traffic Control
CAA	Civil Aviation Authority
CO	Commanding Officer
CSU	Constant Speed Unit
D/F	Direction Finding
EPR	Engine Pressure Ratio
ft	Feet
FTS	Flying Training School
'g'	Gravity, a measure of acceleration
GCA	Ground Controlled Approach
gph	Gallons Per Hour
H/F	High Frequency
hp	Horse Power
HP	High Pressure
IAS	Indicated Air Speed
ICO	Idle Cut Off – fuel/air mixture control
IFR	Instrument Flight Rules
ILS	Instrument Landing System
IMC	Instrument Meteorological Conditions
km/h	Kilometres per hour
lb	Pound (weight and measure of 'boost')
Met	Meteorological
OC	Officer Commanding

PI	Pilot In Command
PPL	Private Pilot Licence
R/T	Radio Telephony
RAE	Royal Aircraft Establishment
RAF	Royal Air Force
RCAF	Royal Canadian Air Force
RFC	Royal Flying Corps
RVR	Runway Visual Range
SBAC	Society of British Aerospace Companies
STOL	Short Take-Off and Landing
UHF	Ultra High Frequency
V2	Take-off safety speed
VFR	Visual Flight Rules
VHF	Very High Frequency
VNE	Velocity Never Exceed
VOR	VHF Omnidirectional Range
Vr	Rotate (for take-off) speed

THE NEIL WILLIAMS
PHOTO ALBUM

Cadet gets flying scholarship badge

Cadet N. M. Williams, of the Cardiff Airport A.T.C. Squadron, was handed his flying scholarship badge last night by Wing-comdr. E. D. Jones, officer commanding No. 1 Welsh Wing of the Air Training Corps.

The scholarship, worth £150 and awarded by the Air Ministry, enables him to train for a civilian pilot's badge. He has already been training with Cardiff Aeroplane Club.

During the ceremony at Pengam Moors Airport, Cardiff, it was stated that the squadron had the highest number of scholarship winning cadets in the Wing.

The award of a Flying Scholarship to Sergeant N. M. Williams of 1344 sqdn ATC

First Solo at 17, in a Tipsy Trainer

A 28-year old Neil Williams waiting his turn to compete in the British International Lockheed Aerobatic Competition, Baginton, Coventry 16th August 1962. The aircraft is one of the four Super Tigers G-ANMZ, 'The Canon'

The British Aerobatic Team at Bilbao in 1964. Left to right: Bob Winter, Peter Phillips, Neil Williams and Team Manager, John Blake. Note the prominent Welsh flag on Neil's overall. Neil flew the Cosmic Wind in Bilbao

Line up of competitors at Little Snoring for the eliminating contest to select the British Team heading for Russia in 1966. Left to right: Neil Williams Team Captain (winner on Zlin 226); Tony Haig-Thomas; Charles 'Taff' Taylor; Barry Tempest and Bob Winter

Neil Williams in an Arrow Active ll, one of his favourite aeroplanes, leading a Tiger Club 'Balbo' of Tiger Moths and Stampes over Central London, photographed from a Super Tiger

The Shuttleworth Collection Sopwith Pup with two pilots and the aircraft restoration team in Royal Flying Corps attire. Neil stands in front of the propeller boss with Des Penrose, ex-De Havilland test pilot on his left. Des Penrose owned, restored and displayed two air racing classics, the Arrow Active Mk. ll G-ABVE, and the Percival Mew Gull G-AEXF, for several years

A Tiger Club formation trio with Stampe leading pictured from a Super Tiger as they pull up into a loop. Neil is flying Super Tiger G-ANZZ

The Daily Telegraph / Neil Williams Trophy awarded annually to the Unlimited British National Champion by the British Aerobatic Association. Winners include Philip Meeson; Peter Kynsey; Nigel Lamb; Mark Jefferies; Diana Britten and Alan Cassidy.

The Trophy was designed by Neil's brother, Lynn Williams, and made by Lynn and friends

INDEX

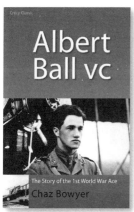

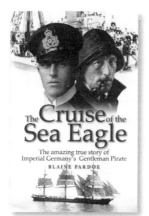

Albert Ball VC
Chaz Bowyer
Fascinating story of the Royal
Flying Corps' first celebrity ace
with 44 kills.
280pp soft cover
Over 75 b&w photographs
9 780947 554897 £10.95

The Cruise of the Sea Eagle
The story of Imperial Germany's
Gentleman Pirate
Blaine Pardoe
Felix von Luckner, the Imperial
German navy raider of WW I.
272 pages, paperback
Approx 30 b&w photographs
9 780859 791205 £10.95

Echoes in the Air
True aviation ghost stories
Jac k Currie
A compilation of researched
aviation ghost stories, famous
and newly discovered,
accompanied by illustrations,
diagrams and photographs.
240 pages paperback
Illustrated throughout
9 780859 791632 £10.95

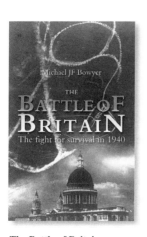

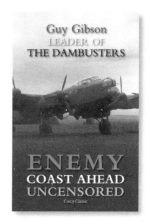

The Battle of Britain
The Fight for Survival in 1940
Michael JF Bowyer
The Battle of Britain day-by-day,
detailing squadrons, aircraft,
locations and people.
240 pages, paperback
Over 120 b&w photographs
9 780859 791472 £10.95

Eagles of the Third Reich
Men of the Luftwaffe in WWII
Samuel W Mitcham Jr
The leaders and pilots
of the Luftwaffe.
320 pages, paperback
51 b&w photographs and 8 maps
9 780859 791496 £10.95

**Enemy Coast Ahead –
Uncensored**
Leader of the Dambusters
Wing Commander Guy Gibson
One of the most outstanding
accounts of WWII.
288 pages, soft cover
b&w photographs and
illustrations throughout
9 780859 791182 £10.95

In the Skies of Nomonhan
Japan versus Russia - September 1939
Dimitar Nedialkov
A new perspective on this interesting and largely unknown pre World War II encounter.
160 pages, soft cover
Over 50 b&w photographs and 20 colour profiles
9 780859 79152 6 £10.95

Janusz Zurakowski
Legend in the Skies
Bill Zuk and Janusz Zurakowski
A rare combination of skilled engineer, painstaking test pilot and unparalleled display pilot.
336 pages, soft cover
Over 75 b&w photographs
9 780859 79128 1 £10.95

Pure Luck
Alan Bramson
An authorised biography of aviation pioneer Sir Thomas Sopwith, 1888-1989
Foreword by HRH The Prince of Wales
288 pages, soft cover
Over 90 b&w photographs
9 780859 791069 £10.95

Fist from the Sky
Peter C Smith
The story of Captain Takashige Egusa the Imperial Japanese Navy's most illustrious dive-bomber pilot
272 pages, soft cover
Over 75 B+W photographs
9 780859 79122 9 £10.95

The Luftwaffe Fighters'
Battle of Britain
Chris Goss
An insight into the experiences of the German fighter and bomber crews from the attacker's viewpoint.
208 pages, soft cover
Over 140 photographs
9 780859 791519 £10.95

Sigh for a Merlin
Testing the Spitfire
Alex Henshaw
The enthralling account of Alex Henshaw's life as a test pilot with the Spitfire.
240 pages, soft cover
b&w photographs throughout
9 780947 554835 £10.95

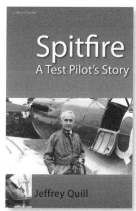

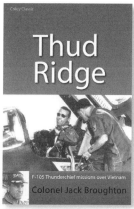

Spitfire
A Test Pilot's Story
Jeffrey Quill
The autobiography of an
exceptional test pilot and RAF
and Fleet Air Arm fighter pilot.
336 pages, soft cover
b&w photographs throughout
9 780947 554729 £10.95

Thud Ridge
Jack Broughton
F-105 Thunderchief missions
over the hostile skies of North
Vietnam
288 pages, soft cover
79 photographs plus maps and
plans
9 780859 791168 £10.95

Winged Warfare
William Avery ('Billy') Bishop
VC, DSO MC
A unique autobiographical and
contemporary account of one of
the highest scoring fighter aces
of World War I.
224 pages, soft cover
integrated b&w photographs
9 780947 554903 £10.95

Stormbird
Hermann Buchner
Autobiography of one of the
Luftwaffe's highest scoring
Me262 aces.
272 pages, soft cover
140 b&w photographs and 16
page colour section
9 780859 791404 £10.95

We Landed By Moonlight
Hugh Verity
Secret RAF Landings in France
1940-1944
256 pages, soft cover
b&w photographs throughout
9 780947 554750 £10.95

Order online at **www.crecy.co.uk**
or telephone +44 (0) 161 499 0024

Crécy Publishing 1a Ringway Trading Est,
Shadowmoss Rd, Manchester, M22 5LH
enquiries@crecy.co.uk